CONVERSATIONS WITH GIO

LIFE-CHANGING LESSONS FROM FATHER TO SON

COACH PAUL THEO

"In *Conversations with Gio*, Theo explores the most fundamental issues of parenthood and the lessons we seek to pass on to our children. Anyone who's spent any time with Theo understands his incredible faith, authenticity, warmth, compassion, energy, and enthusiasm for life. Through his actions and now his book, Theo continues to inspire me to become a better parent to my daughters."

CHRIS ANTONETTI GENERAL MANAGER, CLEVELAND INDIANS
(FAR MORE IMPORTANTLY, DAD OF MYA AND ELLA)

"My Mother always said "Let Go Let God". That is what Life is all about. Not you, but rather God! A God who is loving, kind and merciful. A God who is ALL forgiving. He is my road map in Life. Map Quest God and you get the path of how to reach Him... Not the shortest path to follow, but the hardest path. The path that is not about you, but is about Him! Theo drills home this message in this book to his son. A must read for everyone."

JUDGE JOHN J. RUSSO CLEVELAND, OH

"In a world of children abandoned by their fathers, Paul Theodore offers a powerful, motivating, and refreshing legacy to his son and example to the rest of us. Little Gio will treasure this book as he grows and every father will benefit from it as they contemplate the legacy they want to leave their own children. "Life is not about you" is a strikingly poignant mantra that resonates in our world and will direct you in embracing it as the mindset God has designed for all of us!"

PASTOR STEVE STRONG GRACE BAPTIST CHURCH, WESTLAKE, OH

"Theo has taught so many children and adults to live life to the fullest. To have fun. To not stress. To be the best you can be. He not only teaches this, he lives it. It is evident his true love is family, and he teaches and treats his clients like family. Theo has opened up my life, he has encouraged his clients to be #game-changers, and so many have landed that title on his gym's game-changing wall. *Conversations with Gio* is from the heart, a real life guide to raising a son. It speaks to us in so many real life ways."

MO LOESCH FAMILY FRIEND AND MOTHER OF TWO SETS OF TWINS

"This book is an amazing legacy of love from a father to his son. However, Theo's message is much more FIERCE—this book is about God's LOVE for ALL of us. *"I am the vine. You are the branches."* (John 15:1-17). An excellent addition to everyone's must-read list."

MARIE FIDELA PARAISO, MD PROFESSOR OF SURGERY, CLEVELAND CLINIC LERNER COLLEGE OF MEDICINE
DIVISION HEAD, UROGYNECOLOGY AND RECONSTRUCTIVE PELVIC SURGERY

"There are people who talk to hear themselves talk. Then there are the few who walk the walk. Paul Theodore does just that, not to be noticed by those around them, but to be present for them. Coach Theo's infectious energy makes it impossible for kids everywhere to not gravitate toward him. While some look at the negativities of the world and throw their hands up in disgust and judgment, Theo sees the ability to change the lens we look through. "It's Not About Me" is not just his slogan; it's the motto of his life, his actions and his response to living out his "dash."

NOREEN WOIDKE FAMILY FRIEND AND MOTHER OF THREE

"Gio, a few weeks back I held you in my arms. You trusted me and just stayed there facing away from your parents. In time, your right arm left my neck and pointed in the direction of your father. You knew he was there though you could not see him. You knew his voice and you knew that you wanted eventually to get to him.

Hang on to that instinct. Listen to the counsel of your mother and father, watch their lives, know you are loved. Likewise, listen to the counsel your heavenly Father and let your heart, your mind, your strength and will be directed toward Him. Know that you are loved."

PASTOR TOM MACMILLAN JOHN KNOX PRESBYTERIAN CHURCH, NORTH OLMSTED, OH

DEDICATION

To my wife Amber: You are my life. You gave me a chance when I did not have one. If it were not for you this book would not be possible. Literally. You taught me how to read and write for crying out loud! I love you.

To Gio: I plan to teach you these lessons as you grow up. If for some reason, though, God were to take me from you early, I need you to have these words of love, encouragement, and devotion. It's my assurance that I fulfilled my obligation as your father. I love you.

LIFE IS NOT ABOUT YOU

"Do nothing out of selfish ambition or vain conceit. Rather, in humility value others above yourselves, not looking to your own interests but each of you to the interests of the others."

PHILLIPIANS 2:3-5 (NIV)

ACKNOWLEDGMENTS

There are so many people to acknowledge for making this book possible. In fear of leaving someone out, I choose not to mention names, but to thank everyone who has come into my life to shape, dent, and mold me into the person I am today. I thank God most importantly, for orchestrating it all.

There are five people who I must publicly thank: Anthony Zart, for your amazing talent and design work and Susan Miklaski, Jen Kappler, Nanci Ickes, and Larry Montgomery for reviewing, editing, and enhancing the clarity and quality of this book. I called in a time crunch, and you answered unselfishly. For you all, I'll be forever grateful.

PREFACE

I turned a page and it fell on the floor in front of me. Looking down at the small brown piece of paper, I could make out the image of a church and knew immediately it was a note from my father.

Before I lifted it off the floor and unfolded the page a power was present. The emotion reverberating inside me felt so small and yet like a hurricane all at once. My father had passed away several years before, and like many young men I had carelessly dismissed so many of the greatest gifts he gave me... his words. I still had the pocket knives, the shoe shine kit, some old golf balls and an assortment of tools.

But as the years wore on, the memory of his words, his wisdom, began to fail me. I would find myself hurtling home late at night, the silence of the road beside me, longing to hear his voice...to hear him say my name. I wondered often what he would think of the man I had become.
And here, in a moment, his voice came to me again on a printed page. Like a gift from God.

I held my breath, stooped to pick it up, and unfolded the small, brown piece of paper. I see my name written in his hand and it is too much. The familiar swoop and curl of his beautiful cursive pressing my name on a piece of paper and I am undone. At almost forty years old, I am astonished at the power, the gravity this man still holds in my life.

My father.

Writing my name.

Somewhere behind a desk.

His list of to-do's included me.

Yet I was so far away.

He was thinking of me.

Praying for me.

Writing to me.

Similarly, what you hold in your hands is a note from a father to a son. Ok—it's a rather long and in-depth note, but a note nonetheless. I imagine it would be easy for some to think this is a manual on how you should live your life or father your child. I am certain there are those who will wisely choose to merely adopt the phrases and acronyms throughout the pages. Others will simply read the stories and wonder how one man could be so moved, so compelled to undertake a task this large for his son, a boy of just three years at the time of completion.

But to view this as a manual or a self-help book on fathering would be to miss the point. This is a love letter. A mission. A calling. A rare chance to hear a father say things we long to be said to us. Things we long to be said of us.

You are brave.

You are beautiful.

I believe in you.

Another Father wrote a love letter long ago. Your Father. My Father. The One True Father. He spoke the words we long to be said to us. He spoke the words we long to be said of us.

You are brave.

You are beautiful.

I believe in you.

I find it amazing that tucked inside the story of Jesus is a passage where God the Father knows his son needs to hear his voice. The man who knows all, sees all and creates all is longing for His Father.

The moment Jesus came up out of the baptismal waters, the skies opened up and he saw God's Spirit. It looked like a dove—descending and landing on Him. And along with the Spirit, a voice: *"This is my Son, chosen and marked by my love, delight of my life."* (Matthew 3:16, 17 MSG)

I love that. How beautiful that God chose to include this incredible scene as part of the gospels. A story that models to us that love is never meant to be assumed or insinuated. The Father speaks to the Son. He validates him publicly. He wants him to hear, unashamedly said, that He is not simply a genetic result or a cosmic consequence. The father says He has been chosen, marked, and is the delight of His life.

Stop. Have those words ever been spoken to you?

So many of us walk through life and those words, that message, is dimmed, muted or absent in the clattering chaos of life in America. Shiny cars, scrub-polished models and superstar athletes dwarf any idea of self-worth many of us possess. Absentee parents chasing the next raise, the next thrill, the next purchase have left a generation of children finding answers on television, social media and from anyone that might give them the smallest morsel of attention.

So many of us are asleep. We are asleep so we can dream the American Dream. In our dreams we are raising the next #1 draft pick, straight-A students, corporate CEOs, prom queens and MVPs. In our sleep, we are blind to the fact that a war is raging all around us for the souls of our children and for each other.

We are a nation of parents willing to spend thousands on making our children the athletes or students we want them to become, but we won't spend five minutes asking God what dream He has for their life. We won't take the time to give them permission to fail, to stumble from time to time, forgetting to offer them our support and unconditional love. We won't fall to our knees and pray for the courage to allow God to write the story as He sees fit. The story that He planned from before time began. And how many of us have never simply stopped, looked our child in the eyes and said, "If I could choose...if the world was wide open and I could have any child, just any one kid to share my life with...I'd pick you. A million times over and twice on Sunday, I'd always pick you."

I hope that in the end you will know that this book is an act of bravery and an act of obedience. The gift Theo has given to Gio and to us is a midnight raid into the dark kingdom of lost young men and women longing to find some courage, some resolve to forge a way out of the darkness and back into the light. It is more than simply one man speaking to his son. Rather, Theo is speaking to a generation through Conversations with Gio. He is speaking to the immense need for men and women to begin conversations with their children, even at such a young age. Not simply conversations about education planning, sports accomplishments or financial goals. These and many other topics are plentiful in the world. Instead, he chooses to blatantly move the conversation from this kingdom (the earth) to the kingdom of God. One man who will stand and say 'God first. His will, His way, always.'

As a father, Theo understands clearly that despite his undying love for his children, he cannot give them the one thing they need the most: the story, the salvation God has for their life. He understands that the struggles they will face isn't one of *"flesh and blood"* but a literal battle against the forces of darkness (Ephesians 6:12).

And Theo understands more than anything that the time is now. Not tomorrow. Not when we've read all the right books. Not when we've polished everything up. The time is now to begin pointing them toward God's dream. The time to say 'I love you. GOD loves you.' is now. Right now, in whatever way he may have gifted you.

My father's note was short. He had tucked it inside a book he wanted me to read. However, gone now was the book and in its place a simple, small brown piece of paper remained. He wrote of how great it was to have me home. He urged me not to neglect my church attendance or time spent with God's Word. He joked about me beating him in tennis, and he vowed to improve.

And in the end he wrote seven words that I can barely repeat. I can scarcely say them aloud. Seven words written like a promise and a prayer to a young man who often loses his way and wonders if these words could ever be spoken of him. Seven words that pull me up and push me forward and help me to remember that there is a reality I cannot see with my eyes but I know in my heart.

Seven simple words: 'You are greatly loved by this father.'

Reading his words every time is the same. Something beautiful breaks inside me when I know that just like Jesus... I am chosen, marked, the delight of my father's life.

Cracks and fissures spread along my ribcage and as the tears fall so does my father's love. His love falls all over me, and I am reminded that love is not meant to be held. Love is to be spoken, shared, and spilled.

What I have learned from my father's life, that note, this book and most importantly, from Jesus, is that I must go and do the same. I want to be a father of children who know. They know my hopes and dreams for their lives are that they follow God's hopes and dreams for their lives. They know that I'm crazy about them. Everything. Their smile. Their laugh. The dimples God pressed into their cheeks. The clumsy way they almost trip all the time. They know that when I die, that box they throw me in will be empty because I've left all that I have to say and give them right here. Broken and spilled out just like the greatest father of all time, my father God, did for me.

And that they KNOW...

If I could have a choice...if the world was wide open and I could have any child, just any one kid to share my life with...I'd pick them. A million times over and twice on Sunday. I'd always pick them.

I hope if you learn nothing else from Conversations with Gio, you learn that. Go, spill God's love all over someone's life—certainly the lives of your children. Write the note. Make the call. Stop by the house. Love 'em till it hurts. Fill up their jars and drawers. Stuff their days with it and slip it inside the story of their lives.

Because maybe, just when they need it most, long after you're gone and the words and wisdom begin to fail, they'll turn a page and it will fall on the floor in front of them.

JOHN JACOBS
Sheffield Village, Ohio

INTRODUCTION

You were brought into this world after twelve hours one Tuesday night. On April 7, 2010, your mom labored in agony. I watched in amazement. We both fell to our knees in gratitude. Since that day you have changed my life tremendously. Here's my attempt to change yours.

This book is all about perspective. Once it changes, so does your life. I recall growing up as a child with a false one. Blame it on television, on listening to mainstream culture, or on my own ignorance and lack of comprehension. My perception of reality was skewed, confused, but typical.

The message I heard was that the American Dream was about getting rich, getting everything you want in life, getting until there is nothing else to get. Actually, you can't get enough. That the quest for power and control is what made you worthy. That you work hard so you can play harder, and if you don't have things then you don't have pleasure.

Then I grew up. I discovered just the opposite. Life is about buying less and enjoying it more. Reducing our possessions and enhancing our values. Making a life and not just a living. Adding life to our years and not just years to our life. This can only be accomplished when your quest in life is not for pleasure, or for power, but for meaning.

It is the universal question all humans ask, what is the meaning of my life? Even though I'm just a common man, living a common life, doing common things, I have uncommonly sought out the answer. And here is what I've found:

True meaning comes from living for something far greater than yourself. Life is really not about you at all.

I know that's not easy to hear. I am hitting you with something hard, something that would prevent most people from even turning the pages. But it is the most transformative, life-changing concept I have ever discovered. One that the greatest minds had, have, and will have. One that you need to grasp before you ever proceed to succeed in the game of life. You will not get this in school. Coaches won't train you on it. Employers won't orient you to it. Pastors rarely talk about it. So I write this message to you, loud and clear.

Life. Is. Not. About. You. Period. No question mark. No ifs, ands, or buts to follow. It is not about your desires, your luxury, or your comfort. You wake up each day with a mission to be the best you can be, for everyone around you.

For those that need you.

For those who can't.

For the One who gave you life.

Before you flip the pages, hear me say this. You have so much potential. You can accomplish anything you put your mind to. You will get anything you need in life, as long as you help enough other people get what they need first.

I love you, son. I believe in you. Now get out there and move mountains. Make the world rumble. And create the impact you were meant to create today. You're an absolute game-changer.

He left this world after six hours one Friday night. Over 2,000 years ago Jesus lost His life for us. It is our duty to now lose ours for Him, and everyone out there who desperately needs us.

THE GIRL FROM THE PROJECTS

—

Running through a cemetery, I stop to look at the tombstones.

Standing on top of those that once lived like me, grips me. I imagine they had the same struggles, same concerns, same dreams; just in a different time, to a different degree, and in a different setting.

I look at the years. 1875. 1902. A gentleman who lived 85 years. A little one who lived not so many. Some lived long. Some lived short. But all separated by the same thing.

A dash.

I wonder…

How did they use it? Did they love? Were they loved? Did they dream? Did they accomplish them? How did they live their dash? How am I living mine?

I think back to a story I thank God for. For if he had not put that little girl in my life ten years ago, I would not be living the life that I am today.

I never did learn her name. She was five, maybe six years old with brown hair and chestnut eyes. I met her in the projects of Youngstown on summer break from college. I landed this construction job from a buddy and was simply grateful for the work and a break from the pressure of college. I was making some huge mistakes in my life. I was piling up debt that I had no intention of paying back. I was skipping class to pound beer and grip my controller in endless battles of video game marathons. I was failing school and more importantly failing at life.

I was broke, confused and on a road to nowhere. I was lost.

And in my wandering God placed the little girl with no name right smack dab in my path. Her mom's name was Billy Jean. Billy Jean was a crack-addict, something she admitted to me in a love letter asking me out on a date.

This little girl never said a word. She was quiet and reserved and barely changed her facial expression from the still face she usually wore. Billy Jean decided to prove it to me one day when she said, "Watch, she won't even cry when I smack her face."

Smack. No tears. Not even a frown.

She didn't cry alright. She was emotionally numb. I stared frustrated and irritated, wishing Billie Jean was a male so I could smack her back. For days I tried to imagine what this little child's numbness felt like. Eventually, I did have a breakthrough moment with her.

One day, I was digging up a piece of sidewalk in front of her unit. She was a few feet away watching, as she commonly did. As I pulled the slab of cement from the dirt I found a yellow, toy figurine buried beneath it. I waved her over as I cleaned it off. I knelt down, reached out and said, "Here you go, looks like we found some treasure." She cautiously reached out to receive the gift. She then looked up with her chestnut-colored eyes looking into mine, and a huge smile took over her face.

I never saw her smile before and I would never see it again.

But for her to pull a smile out of her dark, hurtful world, helped me realize that there is hope. The sooner we turn our "me-centered" world into a "God-centered" one, the sooner that hope for her, and every other child that lives in this world, becomes a reality.

God used that little girl, and all the other children that I have worked with over the years for that matter — to teach me the most important lesson in my life…

LIFE IS NOT ABOUT ME.

That's not easy to grasp. But it's the most profound, life-changing truth I have ever learned. And the reason why I can run out of that cemetery living my dash to the fullest today.

In one of my favorite books called, *One Month To Live*, Chris Shook writes, "You get to choose how to spend that little dash of time between the two dates of your earthly existence. What are you spending yours on?

Are you living the dash, knowing fully who you are and why you're here? Or dashing to live, hurriedly spending precious time chasing things that really don't matter to you?"

Life is not about you. There are not many things you control in life; but you do get to control how you use your dash. Control yours, not just for your sake, but for all those still above ground.

I love you, son. I believe in you. Now choose how to live your dash today. It's an absolute game-changer.

ON THE BRINK OF DIVORCE

Your mom was convinced she was through. I had my bags packed with one foot out the door. We were in a black hole. At one-year old, you were growing, our business was growing, but our marriage relationship wasn't. We stopped putting each other first.

It's the tough part that great relationships go through to build resiliency. Relationships based on the wrong thing end on a bad note—divorce, separation, the greener side. Thankfully, our marriage was based on the right thing, faith. Putting God first is what pulled us through. One day while I was mowing the lawn, the vision comes. Your mom is at the store. You are napping. I am in the backyard griping as I cut strips in the yard.

Here is my mental conversation: "Who does she think she is? She has no right to act like this is my fault. I'm doing everything right. I make sacrifices to put her and Gio first. Most guys put football, the stock market, and hanging out with their buddies before their families. They stare at the garbage tube while their wife prepares Sunday dinner. They are at the bar slamming brews while Suzie is at home with the kids. She doesn't realize what she has; I'm not changing anything."

Then I check myself, "Cancel. God." It is a switch phrase I use. Once I say it, old Theo's thoughts get pushed out while the new Theo's thoughts flow in.

Then I heard it. "Shut up. This is not about you. She needs to feel loved. Now show it. Mow 'I love you' in the yard and get over yourself." Arghhh. So I obliged.

Your mom came home from the store, walked down the driveway to the backyard as I finished the rest of the lawn, and froze. For some reason that little message in the yard hit her harder than anything. She melted. And the conversation that was needed started flowing.

It took me many hard-knock lessons to get to the point where I could shut myself down and take a look from the outside.

Here are four of those lessons in particular to live by:

1. LEARN
Learn that I don't know everything and I have a lot to learn. It takes some humility to recognize this. But the learning process in life is a journey, not a destination. So I went to work. One of my 2012 goals was to read one book every week for fifty-two weeks. You want to talk about getting one percent better every day. This could hands-down be one of the most life-changing actions steps to do it. I never used to read books. In fact, I don't ever remember reading one before the age of twenty-two. Now, I understand what Ray Bradbury meant when he said, "There are worse crimes than burning books. One of them is not reading them."
Here are my top 10 life books from that year:
- The Greatest Miracle in the World
- Grace
- Just Like Jesus
- Quiet Strength
- Adam's Return
- Good to Great, In God's Eyes
- The Way to Live
- Mindset
- Coaching the Mental Game
- Switch
- Fearless

2. LISTEN
Wow, what a powerful skill. In counseling it was the skill we were

required to polish most. Then I became a husband, father, fitness coach, business owner; and it was true here as well.

To yourself:

What are you thinking? What are you feeling? What kind of garbage is filling your mind? Are you being rational?

To others:

Be slow to speak and open your ears. What are they feeling? What are they really saying? Is it valid? If they're feeling it, then there must be some validity. Shut your thoughts down and let theirs in. It doesn't mean you have to absorb them. They don't have to fill your emotional tank. You just have to let them in for processing so you can empathize and better relate. And you don't always have to give an answer. That's why listening works. It's sometimes all people want and need.

To God:

We love to talk to him, but how many times do we actually listen!? Stop. Just be. And listen to what He has to say. For me, more often than not, the answers come when I stop asking so many questions.

3. LIFT UP OTHERS

Your mind is boggled. Your stress is rising. The cobwebs are being threaded in your mind faster than you can get dressed and out the door. Find someone and praise them immediately. Give them a compliment. Tell them they look nice. Highlight something they did. It takes the focus off of you and puts it on them. Your spirit gets lifted when theirs does.

4. LET GO

Let go of who you used to be. Your past does not define you. So what if you haven't always been the person you wanted to be; it doesn't mean you have to be that way tomorrow. So you messed up in the past; it doesn't have to dictate what you do in the future. Remove the garbage. Release the pain. Reconstruct your character. Move forward in a different direction. God used murderers and thieves, the meek and decrepit, the oppressed and vulnerable; He WILL use you too if you let him.

The message in the yard eventually faded and I wondered if the spark that transpired would also. It's not like our issues were mulched as quick as the grass strands. Flowers didn't blossom as soon as we walked back in the house.

Your mom and I would still hit ruts, and we knew that. The question wasn't whether or not we would hit them, but rather how we were going to get back up quicker than before?

It sure hasn't been from lifting ourselves up, but instead from reaching out and lifting the other one first.

Life is not about you. You don't always need something fancy to prove it. Just a lawn mower and some grass can do the trick.

I love you, son. I believe in you. Now get out there and cut "I love you" in the lawn today. It's an absolute game-changer.

WASH THEIR FEET

I walked in with my crew after a long day of work. Stomach growling. Muscles aching. It was time for dinner. Before we could eat, our feet needed washed. I got up, grabbed a bucket of water, then started washing.

No, actually I didn't. I'm not a fan of feet. You're not going to find me heading downtown to wash somebody's dirty, rugged, toe-jam-smelling feet.

But Jesus did. It's one of my favorite stories from the Bible. One that I want to stick with you forever.

Jesus washes his disciples' feet. The story can be found in John 13: 1-17.

After a long day, the group of men came in to get ready for supper. It was the Passover feast and at this time Jesus knew his time had come to leave this world.

Jesus gets up from the dinner table, grabs a basin full of water, and makes his way around the table washing his disciples' feet. He goes to everybody. He doesn't skip someone because they weren't as good of a follower or because they didn't show him respect or because they didn't meet his standards.

He kneels before Peter, the man who will soon deny him three times. He looks at him. You think there's no way he'll wash his feet. This guy literally could have saved His life, but pretended he didn't know him. Nope, Jesus washes his feet.

He goes to Judas, the man who sold his soul to the devil and betrayed

Jesus more than anyone. He's definitely going to skip this chump, right? Nope, Jesus washes his feet.

You know what kind of example this is? It doesn't matter who you are, what role you have, if you're the general manager or the bat boy, you're just as responsible and obligated as anyone to wash other people's feet. After he does all this, Jesus addresses the disciples and explains what he just did. He says, *"Do you understand what I have done for you? You address me as 'Teacher' and 'Master,' and rightly so. That is what I am. So if I, the Master and Teacher, washed your feet, you must now wash each other's feet. I've laid down a pattern for you. What I've done, you do"* (John 13: 12-15, The Message).

This all occurs right before the Roman soldiers bust down the doors to take Jesus to his demise. It's one of His last stories, possibly the most important example He wanted to drill home. The message is clear: don't wait, start washing.

Here are a few life lessons about Helping others:

1. IT'S A NECESSITY
The second you realize that life is not about you, and it is about helping other people, is the second your life becomes that much more meaningful and worthwhile to live. There are people out there who need you. You have no time for pity parties or "poor me" attitudes. When you wake up and start your morning you need to ask yourself, who needs me today? Who can I be there for? Who can I reach out to? This is the type of thinking that puts you in action mode, in the driver's seat, and on offense in the game of life.

2. KEEP IT SIMPLE
It doesn't always have to be a grandiose thing that you come up with to try to solve the world's problems either. It's the little things that make a BIG difference. Like helping a new student feel welcome on his or her first day of school, helping your friend with homework, or helping an elderly lady cross the street.

3. GIVE YOUR TIME

Truthfully, the best gift you can ever give is a portion of yourself. Reach out your hand, give your shoulder, lend an ear. You would be surprised at how powerful something as listening is. *"Rings and jewels are not gifts, but apologies for gifts. The only true gift is a portion of thyself."* (Ralph Waldo Emerson-a famous essayist, poet, and lecturer in the 1800's).

4. NOT EVERYONE WANTS IT THOUGH

As a social worker I learned this real fast. I wanted to save everybody. But not everyone wanted it. Even if they said they did, no matter what resources or help was given, they didn't use it right. There are people who do it to themselves. They dig their own deep holes. Honestly, no matter what you do or say, they don't want to be unburied. You can only help people who want to be helped. Be aware and cognizant of this so you're not gullible and taken advantage of. But if you're called to a situation to serve others, even if they don't deserve it, do it anyways. Don't worry about where their heart is. If God wants you to do it, then keep your heart in the right place.

5. BE PROACTIVE ABOUT IT

Ask not what your friends can do for you, but what you can do for your friends. Don't wait to be reached out to, instead do the reaching out. Pray not for what God can do for you, but what you can do for Him.

6. YOU WILL PROSPER

A funny thing happens when you give, you will receive. Now that's not why you do it. That's just a fringe benefit, a perk, a bonus for doing it. You should always give without any intention of receiving anything in return. But don't be surprised when you're blessed for it.

"Whoever wants to be great must become a servant. Whoever wants to be first among you must be your slave. That is what the Son of Man has done: He came to serve, not to be served—and then to give away his life in exchange for the many who are held hostage." (Matthew 20:26-28, The Message).

Even Jesus, King of Kings, God in the flesh, the CEO, the head coach, the grand master, didn't come on this earth to be served, but to serve. Whether you want to or not, you should do the same.

Life is not about you. Grab a basin of water and begin making your way around the room. Heck, you might just notice that your feet become naturally clean in the process.

I love you, son. I believe in you. Now get out there and start washing others' feet today. It's an absolute game-changer.

WHY TRAIN

—

Rocky Balboa changed my life. The 80's boxing icon couldn't be defeated. He beat Apollo Creed, Hulk Hogan, Mr. T, the Russian, Tommy Gunn, always as an underdog too. He had heart, mental grit, and a body made of steel.

He had me working out in sixth grade too. After watching him defeat Drago (the Russian) in his fourth movie, he inspired me to train like a champ. At twelve years old, I started running laps around the house, lifting my dad's rusted out weights in the garage, and even turned shoveling snow into an intense workout routine.

I wanted to be strong. I wanted to be mentally tough. I wanted to outlast anybody. But what started out as a desire to follow the Italian stallion up the Philadelphia staircase turned into a serious body image disorder. I became so obsessed with my physical appearance, that it became more important than my spiritual growth. I wanted to be ripped. I wanted to look like the guys on the cover of Men's Health magazines.

There's nothing wrong with wanting to look good. But when it becomes your core reason for training, then you have a problem. The fitness industry likes to make it all about looking good. Misleading advertisements convey that when you get 6-pack abs, bulging biceps, and look good in the mirror, then you'll be happy.

Those may be perks and benefits for all your hard work. But anything out of selfishness or vanity never truly fulfills nor produces lasting motivation. I had to find a different reason for training.

A greater cause. Something bigger than me. Something more than my own life.

WHY TRAIN?

1. FOR THOSE WHO CAN'T

There are a lot of people out there who wish they could use their bodies: kids in wheelchairs, soldiers with missing limbs from combat, moms battling cancer. They wish their bodies were able. We run because our legs work. We lift weights because our muscles are able. We do this BECAUSE WE CAN.

2. FOR THOSE WHO NEED US

Training helps us get better in all aspects of life. Our minds become stronger, our attitudes more positive, our spirit more enduring. But it's not just for us to enjoy the fruit of our labor. It's for those around us. Our wives need us to rise up. Our children are watching. The world is crumbling. We do this to get better FOR THEM.

3. FOR THE ONE WHO GAVE US LIFE

God gave us the greatest gift in the world; the gift of life. We show appreciation by taking care of it. We don't take care of our body to earn his love; it's because He loves us and because He gave us this body that we take care of it.

Once you see the bigger picture you begin to gain a different motivation — a type that lasts. You realize there's no more time for pity parties. It doesn't matter if you want to do it or not. People need you. We train hard for them.

I still like to train hard like Rocky, but not just for the abs of steel. I do it because I want to be a strong leader in my household. I do it because I want to outlast my wife and children; so I can serve and protect them as long as they live. I do it to change my life, so when I get outside those gym walls, I can change the lives of others.

Life is not about you. Put purpose and intention behind your training so you don't let building a stronger physique interfere with building a stronger heart.

I love you, son. I believe in you. Now get out there and train for something greater than yourself today. It's an absolute game-changer.

RUN AGAINST TRAFFIC

*"The only place success comes before
work is in the dictionary."* —Vince Lombardi

On a cold winter night during my freshman year of high school, a six-teen- year-old neighbor lost her life. She was walking with traffic on a local, main road. A car slammed into her from behind. She didn't even see it coming.

I do not recall if anyone actually told me, but I learned quickly to run against the flow of traffic during my high school wrestling days. When-ever I would head out for a training run, I would stay on the opposite side of the street. I preferred to dodge the cars coming toward me rather than trust that those behind would see me. My fate felt safer, wiser, and more controlled this way. Running against traffic on the road seemed easy. In life, it's much more difficult.

It takes hard work. Thank God my dad taught me the value of it. He has always been a hardworking blue-collared, Italian man. This is a guy who has worked in a factory most of his adult life. Prior to that he worked in a grocery store and raised a family of four on minimum wage. Before he entered the family life, he served his country loud and proud as a sergeant for four years in the United States Marine Corps. I never saw him miss work or turn down overtime. I never heard him complain about it either.

My dad could have had more, but he made sacrifices for his family. He tells a story of his post-Marine days. He was able to get a job working for the Federal Government, but it would have required re-location to another state. My mother didn't agree with that because it required her to leave family. So my dad declined the Federal job, and his menial job barely making ends meet, he accepted. Hard work became a necessity, not just a choice, for my dad. He proved that even if you don't have much to show for hard work, you can't get very far without it.

Here are some lessons my dad taught me about hard work:

1. HARD WORK IS NOT AN OPTION
There is no substitute for success. "The only time success comes before work is in the dictionary." (Lombardi) Too often people look for the easy route. A six-year degree in one year, a six-figure salary in one month, a six-pack of abs in one day.

We see this mentality a lot in the fitness world. People want results, but they're not willing to put forth the effort to achieve them. If takes time to get it, then it's not worth the time. But don't let this world fool you. There's no quick and easy fix, there's no magic pill, there's no overnight success story.

Your mom and I started our business in the backyard with three kids. At one point we went two months without any income. We went through our entire savings to get our vision going. Three years later we moved into our own 6,000-sq ft facility, with over hundreds of people in our programs on a weekly basis. If we would have stopped when the going got tough, we would have never been going, anywhere.

2. HARD WORK BEATS TALENT WHEN TALENT STOPS WORKING
There will be those select people who do get things the easy way — whether it be natural-born opportunities or natural-born gifts and abilities. They'll frustrate you when they nail things on the first try. In fact, you may even be one of them. Know that it will only get you so far if you're not priming and polishing your efforts with constant work and dedication. The cream of the crop eventually rises to the top in life from hard work, not from talent alone.

Take Michael Jordan for example. An iconic athlete, heralded as the best professional basketball player in the history of the NBA. Jordan won six national championships and six MVP titles during his stint with the Chicago Bulls. But the coolest part about his story is that he wasn't always the top player. In fact, he didn't even make the varsity squad during his sophomore year in high school. He began practicing rigorously to prove his abilities and make the team the following year. His gym coach said that he would find MJ shooting hoops almost every morning before school started, and had to ask him to leave the court almost every time to get to class.

He may have been talented, but Michael Jordan worked hard to build his basketball skills. It paid off. Eventually he earned the number-two slot on the list of top athletes of the century, only behind the legendary baseball player Babe Ruth.

3. DO IT WITH PRIDE

Whether you're flipping burgers, cleaning floors, working with people or computers, *"Do it so well that the living, the dead, and the unborn could do it no better."* (Martin Luther King, Jr.)

Your efforts will be noticed when you least expect it. It will earn you team captain, first chair, the new job you want or a promotion in your current one. Even if no one notices, do it anyways. Work hard not because you want to impress people, or because you want to look good, or earn trophies. Do it because you know it's the only way to reach your highest potential, and help others reach theirs too.

My dad's hard work may not have been recognized by the Today Show, or the Nobel Peace Prize committee, or People magazine. But it was recognized by us. We followed his example through what he did, not by what he said.

4. IF YOU'RE NOT DEAD, YOU CAN'T QUIT

Winston Churchill, a famous British politician, pronounced these six words that have become a commonly recited quote, *"Never, never, never, never give up."*

There's a difference between giving up when you need to, like when you do twenty-five hundred pull ups and snap a bicep tendon, versus giving up when you want to; like when you stop studying for a test because you don't want to try anymore. When you give it everything you have and the decision is rational, it's ok to stop. When you're just being lazy, it's not.

There will be so many times in your life where your mind will want to give up. You can't let it. Your body will do it; you just have to keep pushing your mind through it.

I wanted to quit during wrestling practices.

I wanted to quit during my first marathon.

I wanted to quit when Fit Me Up didn't look like it was going to make it.

I wanted to quit when my marriage was falling apart.

I wanted to quit during the intense workout I just did this morning before I wrote this chapter.

But I didn't, because I knew it would make me better. As long as you're alive, you can't quit. If you do, you'll never find what you're made of.

5. WORK HARD, NOT A LOT

I have to point this out to ensure your priorities are congruent with your values. Midnight shifts didn't stop my dad from coaching our little league teams. Putting forth his maximum effort for eight hours on the clock didn't zap his energy from being with us when he was off. Taking a promotion would have never happened if it meant a reduction from family time.

There's a misconception in this culture that busyness equals productivity. The busier people are the more productive they feel. The sad thing is that many chase productivity as a measure of their self-worth. But being busy and being productive are not the same. Being productive means you're producing something, or yielding or furnishing results. Being busy could mean you're just occupying your time and using up energy.

Working hard produces; working a lot keeps you busy. You can produce quality work in a short amount of time. I always say, "Get in, and get out," so you can spend time on what truly matters in life. There will be times when you'll have to "provide" for your family, so work may take precedence over family time. But if you're providing too much time to your finances and not to your family, eventually you'll leave them in a mental, emotional, and spiritual deficit. That's when it's time to make sacrifices with work and material pleasures, in order to ensure your priorities are straight with your family ones.

What's crazy about my dad's story is that he didn't have a dad to learn from. His father bailed on his family at a very young age, leaving his two brothers and his mother fending for themselves. He fought against many obstacles throughout his life. But it's why he is who he is today—a dad than any child would ask for.

His principles and work ethic are part of a road far less traveled. Not many people will choose his route. But if you're traveling the same way as everyone else, then you're probably in the wrong lane anyways.

Life is not about you. Don't run with the flow of traffic. For if you do, you may not necessarily get hit by a car, but you sure will lose quality of life.

I love you, son. I believe in you. Now get out there and work hard today. It's an absolute game-changer.

FIND A COACH, BE A COACH

Mentorship is powerful. I used to be very involved with a mentorship organization called Big Brothers Big Sisters of Greater Cleveland. Their mission is to match up kids with adult mentors. Their philosophy is that an adult role model can positively change a child's life. Statistics show that this philosophy is right. One of the most powerful, positive influences on a human being's life is the connection with a positive adult role model.

Coaches. We all need them and we all need to be one. *"Iron sharpens iron, and one man sharpens another."* (Prov 27:17)

Leaders Follow

You can't be a good leader without first learning how to follow. I used to think I could do it on my own. I learned real fast that that wasn't getting me far. And when I looked around at some very successful people, I noticed that they all had coaches. If you want to get to the next level, you need one.

There are all kinds of them. There are athletic coaches. Professional coaches. Fitness and nutrition coaches. Financial coaches. Depending on where you are, you may need a few of them.

If you're a Christian and you want to take your walk to the next level, you NEED a Disciple Coach. It's an absolute must. It has to be someone different than your father or mother too. They are usually our main coaches in life. But the dynamics is different. We don't always listen to our parents.

Let me tell you about my coach. I signed up with him a few years ago. His name is John Jacobs. Because of him, I had quit my job, lost my savings, and almost my house in the process. But because of him, I also started a business ministry, opened up my own facility, accomplished some paramount fitness goals, saved my marriage, become a better father, and I am living my life to the fullest---walking stronger in my faith than ever before.

Here's why—every time I say I feel like God is calling me to do something, John says DO IT. Whenever I point the finger at my wife and say she needs to change—John points the finger back at me and says no YOU DO.

Coaches will be there when you need them. They'll listen nonjudgmentally. They'll criticize constructively. They'll speak the truth lovingly. But they will also hold you accountable, call you out, and push you past your perceived limitations. They will check you, but you have to let them.

Be Coachable
Having a coach is one thing; being coachable is another. It takes humility. You have to take advice and put it into practice, and you do it because you know it's going to help you be the best you can be, so you can eventually step out and BE, a coach yourself.

Be A Coach
It's the great commission. The last thing Jesus says to his disciples before he descends into heaven is this: *"Go therefore and make disciples of all nations, baptizing them in the name of the Father and of the Son and of the Holy Spirit, teaching them to observe all that I have commanded you."* (Matt 28:18-20)

If I were on my death bed about to leave this earth, the last words that I utter to you will probably be the most important. I would hope you take them seriously.

Never doubt your influence.
He didn't say, "Wait until you're ready. Hold up, you don't have enough success or money yet. You're just not good enough of a follower yet." He

said GO. The words will come. The behaviors will come. You'll know what to do.

The best thing you can do is just be there for someone. I have had many parents thank me for changing their children's lives. One cracked a joke and said I must be a magician. Honestly, my magic is to genuinely care for those that are in my care. I'm not sure I say or do anything special. I'm just there.

Drop your clipboard
I say this because sometimes when I walk into a workout, that's what I have to do. My plan wasn't necessarily what the group or person needed. A situation changed their day or maybe their mood did. As an effective coach your job isn't to worry so much about designing a successful program or formula. It's about successfully being Present. In the moment. Dropping your thoughts and picking up theirs. Relationship building thrives there. And from there, effective coaching does.

Your ministry starts with your family first.
This is a must. If you're not making time to pray with your family, disciple them, and invest in them, then you need to re-prioritize. If that ministry crumbles, then what you do outside with others will eventually too.

Life is not about you. Follow these action steps if you want to get to the next level.

I love you, son. I believe in you. Now find a coach and be a coach today. It's an absolute game-changer.

PLUG INTO PEOPLE

I am not a big fan of garage sales.

I cringe every time your mom asks me to help her with one. Be it the hours it takes to transport everything from the attic to the garage, the eight-hour shifts we sit outside, for three days in a row, or the additional hours it takes to pack the unsold stuff back in the attic or stash it on the curb for trash day. For whatever reason I find it stressful and inefficient use of my time.

But the one thing I do like, and probably the only thing…The one thing that blows my mind every time, and actually gives the garage sale meaning and purpose and reason and why I think God wants me to experience them in the first place… is the people.

You never knew who's going to walk up, and you never know what stories you're going to hear. But at the end of the day, that's what makes me consider it all worthwhile.

The stories. Your mom always finds a way to pull them out. You should watch her in action. She's a true garage sale disciple. Public speaking, she won't have it. Speak to her bible study group, and she's relieved if she finds a way to get out of it. Network in a large group setting at a fitness convention and she'll prefer to go to her room. Perform at a race and she'll get nervous stomach aches for days prior to it. But witness to people at a garage sale, and she's all over it.

There's the story of the hoarder. The nice older lady who pulls up with a four-door sedan stuffed to capacity with collected junk. She admits that she has a problem and further admits that her son actually disowned her for it. He moved away a year ago and hasn't talked to her since. She talks as if she doesn't have a problem and instead as if the problem has her. And your mom and I spend an hour after she leaves trying to wrap our heads around a lady whose compulsion has taken over her life and is ruining it.

Then there's the story of the abused wife. She tells us how she was married once, and then divorced because he was abusive. Then she got remarried, but ended up in a women's domestic violence center after experiencing more abuse. After finally getting back on her feet she ends up living in a two-bedroom apartment with her teenage daughter's baby as she (the teenage daughter) leaves for months at a time to she sells drugs. This lady's face lights up as she excitedly tells us that she's hopeful to finally get off unemployment as she has some potential job opportunities lined up. She recites scripture as she shares her story and praises God for always providing. As she heads down the driveway we tell her we'll pray for her, and are left humbled by her faith through all of the chaos.

Finally, there's the story that truly rocked my world for days. We meet a full-blooded Italian lady, and we immediately hit it off. You rarely meet one of those nowadays! Italians are like family, even if it's your first meeting with each other. She shared with us the story of her teenage son who contracted a rare autoimmune disorder known as Guillain-barre syndrome. Guillain-barre is a serious disorder that occurs when the body's defense (immune) system mistakenly attacks part of the nervous system. This leads to nerve inflammation that causes muscle weakness and other symptoms.

This disorder paralyzed him at age eleven.

Prior to this incident he was a stellar athlete and hockey player. He was quick, strong, and agile. Now, his mom states he can only go to the games and support his friends as he watches them compete on the ice. I shook off the tears as I got choked up.

This young man has worked his way back up to walking with the assistance of braces, and his mom says he's in pretty good spirits, but I can only imagine the hurt he must feel as he watches from the sidelines.

We take for granted the bodies and physical abilities that we have. We make excuses for why we can't get to the gym or go for a run. Here's a guy who would do anything to retain the physicality that he once possessed.

You never know what people are dealing with.

For whatever reason God uses garage sales to drill this point home.

It forces you to be careful about the judgments, assumptions, and first impressions that you make when you first encounter people.

It forces you to think twice about the cashier who doesn't talk and comes off as rude; or the irate driver who speeds through lanes, cuts in front of you, and almost receives the flip of your bird in return; or the child who's distracted in class and you're about to label as defiant.

Maybe she just found emails from her husband to a different woman prior to coming to work; maybe he just got a call that his mother with Alzheimer's is taking her last breath and he races to the nursing home, and maybe this student is thinking about the abuse he's most likely to endure when he gets home from school rather than what you have to write on the chalkboard.

You never know what people are going through.

So what's a solution to all of this... Plug into people. Plug in as in light up, juice up, amplify. Never underestimate what the power of your words, the lending of your ear, and the brace of your shoulder can have. It might be exactly what people are waiting for. I can tell you from my own experience the significant impact this has had on me.

Three distinctive moments in my life when people plugged into me:

1. Ms. Kotsol. It was 7th or 8th grade. I was hanging around trouble-making friends, I started to act like them to be cool like them, and she knew it. She pulled me to the side one day in class and casually said something like, "You shouldn't do what they do, you're better than that." She probably has no idea how profound her words were. "I'm better than that, you see that in me, you really do!" Her words sunk in and penetrated through to my core.

It might have been a few years later that I actually fell back on those words and realized that I could and should be my own person. Out of all the English and reading or whatever she taught me, I don't remember a lick. But that moment she plugged in to me, I'll never forget.

2. John Jacobs. God brought John into my life at one of the most pivotal times and I didn't even know it. Long story short, I was twenty-seven years-old, working at a non-profit in East Cleveland, and just starting to grow strong in my faith. It was because of life group at church that I grew my friendship with Double J. I started getting this nudge to quit my job and pursue our fitness business. It was so new to me at the time that I had no clue how I was going to pull it off. I just knew that I was getting the call. What would my family think? How would people look at me? Where would the money come from? Fear. Fear. And more Fear. No one gave me the answer I wanted to hear, but John. He said, "Bro, if it's what God wants you to do, then do it."

But I think even bigger than this is that John met with me on an occasional basis. He taught me what it means to be a Christian, and he always lifted me up and praised me. He pointed out things in me that I never knew people noticed. He made me feel like I had potential and encouraged me to reach it. If weren't for him, I'd never be living the best life in the world, making money doing what I love, taking chances and doing things that I never thought I could do. All because he plugged into me.

3. David Jack. One of the most well-known fitness coaches in the industry. A contributor to Men's Health, Reebok, and multiple elite fitness organizations across the country. People seek his knowledge and wisdom and especially his public speaking skills. He's one of the best speakers I've ever heard in my life. It was that skill that landed him the emcee role at the International Youth Conditioning Association summit, where I met him two years ago. Why did he take the chance to introduce himself to me after a breakout session? Out of all the other people in the room—call it God-orchestrated. He knew what He was doing and what I needed to hear. For some odd reason after only one or two sentences we both picked up on the fact that we were Christians. And from there we hit it off. We talked about what I was doing, and I shared with him the Fit Me Up logo and mission. He loved it. I shared with him my passion but fears to run with the faith and fitness thing. He shared with me his passion and fears to do the same. We lifted each other up and encouraged each other to keep running with God's plans, not ours.

I left that conference validated and convicted to keep following God's lead and doing what he asks. The opportunities keep popping up. If only D Jack knew how close I was to wavering. Actually he didn't need to know, he just did what he was good at and plugged into me. If he would have held back I would never be where I am today. I left that conference with a wealth of knowledge about youth fitness training and athletic development. But what I recall the most, and thank God for more than anything, was being lit up by D Jack.

So the next time you feel the urge to say something, say it. The next time you sense the hurt of a friend at a gathering, acknowledge it. The next time you feel the absence of love among those in your proximity, spread it. I'm sure these guys don't even realize what they did and at the time, I didn't even realize I was looking for it.

You never know when your plug will release its charge.

Take the story of Melvin, a seventeen year-old who I've had the privilege of working with at a project at an alternative high school called Life Skills. Life Skills is basically for teenagers, ages sixteen through twenty-one, who for various reasons can no longer function in a normal high school setting. Drugs, behavior issues, destructive families, crime, jail, and other things just got the best of them, and now they have a chance to get back on track.

I knew Melvin had something special after the second or third session. He started to come out of his shell, and his work ethic exceeded the rest of the group's. But I didn't know he was listening, and I definitely had no clue the influence I was having.

Until he wrote this testimony...

When Theo came to our school I figured that I should actually listen to what he says, even if I'm not that physically fit. The first few meetings with him really tested my abilities. There were a lot of people in the first few weeks, so I felt that I probably wouldn't fit in. I had a lot of things going wrong; I was on a bad path. Most teenagers would see this program as a joke, at first that's the way I was thinking. It wasn't until the last two meetings before our summer break that I realized that this isn't a joke and Theo is actually serious about helping us.

During our summer break I sported a wristband that I earned with hard work. We had a challenge meeting before our break and the people who met the times/reps, earned a wristband. These wristbands are a system Theo uses in his workouts to show the level you are at (physically). During summer break all I did was brag to my friends about how I earned this wristband. I wear this wristband with pride. The week before we started school again I was put in drug classes because of the trouble I was in. These classes were very hard to handle during break; relapse was constantly on my mind. First week back to school was very hard, all I could think about was smoking even though I couldn't. The first meeting we had with Theo when we got back felt great. I could just workout all of my anger.

The following meetings were getting a little harder so I felt the challenge and took it personally. Theo has been a great motivator through all of these workouts but more importantly he inspired me to remain sober, and to stay in shape. I never thought at the beginning that I would be where I'm at today. To this date I'm seven weeks sober, and I feel great about it. I learned a lot about life and staying fit throughout the past ten to eleven weeks, and most of the thanks I give would have to go to Theo, the others would have to go to select friends and my family. My mom and dad can see how I changed; I'm more confident and look more fit. Now all my friends and family know that I'm not normal, I'm HARDCORE!

Seventeen and seven weeks sober.

For him to contribute even an ounce of acknowledgement to me, blew me away. It's why you need to be on your "A-game" all the time. Be ready to infuse your energy, vitality, and life into everyone you come into contact with. When you walk through the door of a meeting, a class, a service, whatever it may be, get ready to clear your mind and be in the moment.

Life is not about you. Look people in their eyes. Drop your thoughts and pick up theirs. Plug into them. You never know when it will change their life. And more often than not, yours.

I love you, son. I believe in you. Now get out there and plug into people today. It's an absolute game-changer.

WHEN YOU THINK NO ONE'S WATCHING, THINK AGAIN

You came running around the corner one day saying you wanted to workout. I got pumped and encouraged you. You started pulling off your clothes. "What are you doing, Gio; I thought you said you wanted to work out?" "Yea daddy I gotta do a workout in my underwear." "Why do you have to do it in your underwear buddy?" "Because daddy—that's what you do."

When you think no one's watching, your three-year-old starts to strip down. This has been the theme lately. Not that people are taking their clothes off, but that they're watching. The lesson keeps smacking me hard.

Let me tell you about five-year-old Grady. He was at *Pull Ups for Zoë*, a world record pull-up attempt you'll read about later. Six weeks later his mom has caught him numerous of times. Laptop open. *Pull Ups for Zoë* highlight video on. He's doing pull ups on the towel bar in the shower. She text me the video and tears filled my eyes. So inspired. So humbled. So reminded of this fundamental lesson: Never doubt the power of your influence. I can't even imagine what would go through this little boy's head that he would choose to escape his "Sesame Street" world to go into the bathroom and enter the "Theo and Pull Ups for Zoe" zone.

Then there's the child who uses the phrase "game-changer" on their card they made for me. The one who says their favorite quote is "Not dead, Can't Quit" because they saw it at our event.

The one who knows my favorite song because they say they hear me sing it all the time. The one who knew I went to Menchies for fro-yo because they saw it on Facebook.

That's what happens. These young minds are soaking, absorbing, and digesting. Our everyday words, emotions, and actions are being implanted into their heads every single second. And they're ready to model them.

That's why when parents ask how to get their kids to eat healthy—I say, start eating healthy. Get them to be more positive—be more positive. More confident—believe in yourself more.

Why get fit? Maybe because they'll need the inspiration to do it themselves. Do it as a service to alter the course of their lives.

Why give up the cigarettes? Maybe because you don't want them dealing with the same struggle as you may have when they get older. It's a hard habit to kick. Prevent them from getting started in the first place.

Why get to church on Sunday? Because even though you don't know exactly what you believe in yet, you want them to know that at least you're trying to figure it out.

Why give your wife a hug and say you're sorry? Because you want them to learn how to suck up their pride and own up to their mistakes.... whether they like it or not.

Why not flip the driver off who just cut you off? Because you want them to learn patience and understanding that maybe that person has a dire situation to attend to, and they didn't mean to.

Why not disown your teenage son after you find him smoking pot in your house? Because even though you assert that it's completely out of line and unacceptable, you want him to know that you made mistakes too, and the good news is: the forgiven forgive.

Why give up a career path to stay at home more with your family? Because you want them to know how to make sacrifices for a life worth living for.

Why not get divorced even though you think your marriage is beyond repair? Because you want them to know that commitment isn't easy, but it's worth it, through good or bad, sickness and in health, 'til death do you part.

I find this poem fits well:

When you thought I wasn't looking, by Mary Korazan
When you thought I wasn't looking,
I saw you hang my first painting on the refrigerator,
and I wanted to paint another one.

When you thought I wasn't looking,
I saw you feed a stray cat,
and I thought it was good to be kind to animals.

When you thought I wasn't looking,
I saw you make my favorite cake for me,
and I knew that little things are special things.

When you thought I wasn't looking,
I heard you say a prayer,
and I believed that there was a God to talk to.

When you thought I wasn't looking,
I felt you kiss me goodnight,
and I felt loved.

When you thought I wasn't looking,
I saw tears come from your eyes,
and I learned that sometimes things hurt,
but it's alright to cry.

When you thought I wasn't looking,
I saw that you cared,
and I wanted to be everything that I could be.

When you thought I wasn't looking,
I looked...
and I wanted to say thanks for all the things
I saw when you thought I wasn't looking.

You started doing sprints from your easel to the TV stand. Then you started doing burpees. Then jumping jacks. You didn't do it because I told you to; you did it because I showed you to.

Life is not about you. You reminded me that when you think no one's watching, your children are. And they might just pull off their clothes and start doing pushups in the living room one day to prove it.

I love you, son. I believe in you. Now RISE UP and lead by example for all that are watching today. It's an absolute game-changer.

SURROUNDED BY CANCER, WTS

—

One Sunday morning I sat watching you run around our friend Dan's studio. You pulled out the agility ladder, picked up the slam balls, and hung from the pull-up straps. You invited me into your world to participate, and I gladly joined. But the best part for me was sitting back watching, observing, and appreciating your discovery, exploration, and imagination. Tears welled up. It took everything I had to fight them back. I couldn't imagine ever losing this moment.

Ninety minutes earlier I ran through the finish line of a local 5k race with a child whose family has to anticipate the worst. Meet my man Michael Orbany. Eight years-old. Brain cancer for the second time. This little guy is a fighter with a warrior spirit. At first I was supposed to run FOR him. On that Friday night I was plotting a game plan to take the top five for him. Then on Saturday I got the text from a good friend Mo—"What can we push Michael in?" A running stroller, I said, "Who's pushing?" "Will you?," she asked. BAM. It's not about me. "Absolutely." So I ran WITH him.

What. A. Blessing. I was the legs, but he was the spirit, and he kept us moving. He waved to his fans throughout the course. I prayed he didn't get motion sickness from my poor piloting skills. He agreed to turbo speed on the last mile. We had a blast and rocked the race, but I was rocked for the day…emotionally.

It seems like we are surrounded by cancer lately. Everywhere we turn it's intruding on another person's life.

So many people inspiring us:
- Michael's going through his second battle.
- Tracy defeated her first battle but now backs up her husband for his.
- Sean, only nineteen years-old.
- Emily, lost her four year-old Sophie five and a half years ago.
- Our best friend's mom, Nancie.
- Debbie lost her twelve year-old Emily four years ago.

It's not fair. It doesn't make sense. And I don't think we'll ever understand why it happens. We trust that it's all part of His plan, but we don't agree with it. We feel helpless. We want to find a cure. We want to take the pain away. What can possibly be done?

The only thing I can fall back on his having WTS, a Willingness To Serve. You can't control much, but you can control this. Just be ready and be willing. That's all you need. Sometimes we think we're not able. No time, no money, not in the position to do so. Sometimes we think we're not worthy. Not good enough, talented enough, or know enough. But believing these lies will prevent you from doing and experiencing what you were meant to.

Be willing:
To use what you've been given. I can run. I can push a stroller. I used it.
To give up your goals to help another reach theirs. I was shooting to run a 6:15 minute mile, but God had another pace in mind.
To answer the call when it comes in. Wonder if I didn't? Michael wouldn't have missed out, I would have.

I write this not for a pat on the back, but to encourage you to trust that you can play a part. No matter how big or small. Just be willing. That's all that we can do. It's all we have to do.

You may not have much to give, but much isn't required, just your legs and a 180-heart rate for four miles. With one hundred meters left, Michael and I pulled off the track. I helped him get out of the stroller and together we strolled through the finish line. I've finished a lot of races before. But this is the only one I've ever won.

Life is not about you. BE WILLING to admit that.

I love you, son. I believe in you. Now get out there and serve today. It's an absolute game-changer.

THE CHAMPION MENTALITY

—

The score is 7-6. I'm up by one point. If I want to return to the state tournament I have to win this match. How am I beating this guy? He's ranked second in the state. Quite frankly, he doesn't feel that tough, but the predictions say he is. I can easily hold on for one more minute, but that's not how it was expected to play out. Do I deserve this? The anxiety just heightened. I take one more shot in on his legs, but I'm too nervous now to try my signature move. He cranks on my head, spins around, and scores his two points. My junior wrestling season is over.

Wrestling was my sport. I did it for nine years of my life. Actually, it became my life. But while I had many successes, I never reached my potential. Not because I lacked ability or training, but because I lacked the right mindset. I was a head case. The insecurity from this haunted me for many years, sending me on a pursuit to figure out the mental game.

The mind. It can be your worst enemy. But it can also be your best ally. Defeat it and you'll move mountains. Let it win and you'll stand at the bottom looking up. You can be the most talented, most athletic, most likely to win it all, but if you don't have the right mindset, you never will.

I read this illustration in a book one time, "Picture two fighters engaged in combat. After a long tough battle, the one who has been slightly dominant catches the other in a choke hold and begins to tighten the hold… What would you do in that situation?"

If you responded with "I'd fight like heck to get out," your mindset is of the majority, thinking you're the one losing the fight. Not many see themselves as the one doing the choking. It's rare to have this champion mentality.

I've always been intrigued by the champion mentality. The truest test is when faced with death. Could one maintain it when his life is on the line? Just ask Viktor Frankl. Concentration camps. Stripped from his normal life, his wife, his family, his hair, his clothes, and his dignity. Starved and beaten, sick and frost bitten. He could have given up. Most did. In his book Man's Search for Meaning, he tells of how most didn't die from starvation first, but rather a loss of hope. He recounts some of his self-talk to maintain his. He rehearsed speeches he would tell one day, he imagined conversations with his wife, he promised he would never run into the "electric fence."

"This was a phrase used in camp to describe the most popular method of suicide—touching the electrically charged barbed-wire fence. There was little point in committing suicide, since, for the average inmate, life expectation, calculating objectively and counting all likely chances, was very poor....Even the gas chambers lost their horrors for him [inmates] after the first few days—after all, they spared him the act of committing suicide."

Frankl didn't necessarily think he would make it much longer, he just knew he would do whatever he could to survive. And he did. This is the champion mentality. You follow your instincts. You trust your strength. You rely on your perseverance. You fight with everything you've got, regardless of the outcome.

When I ran my first marathon I didn't know how I would finish. Twenty-six miles. Three and a half hours. There's plenty to think about: the nourishment, the mental game, the "wall" that everyone talks about. Once I hit it, could I push through? Honestly, there was no point in even thinking about it. Just do it and see what happens. I focused on my training and trusted that I would give it my best. I took that first step, then a second one, then 26.2 miles of them. I think that's when the truth of confidence finally clicked.

Taking that first step. Sometimes we fail to take it just because we can't see the top of the staircase. We think about the what-ifs, the unknowns, the outcome so much, that we prevent ourselves from moving forward to where we can be. We wait until we're ready, until we get a sign, until the time is right. Sometimes you just have to go and trust that you are capable, and you will find the way. You might trip along the way. You might hit road blocks. But even if you don't make it to the top, you're one step closer to it.

John Wooden proclaimed this philosophy about how daily incremental improvements is what produces true champions. Wooden is acclaimed as one of the most successful college coaches in NCAA history. He took his UCLA basketball team to ten national titles in twelve years. I take his words seriously. "When you improve a little each day, eventually big things occur. When you improve conditioning a little each day, eventually you have a big improvement in conditioning. Not tomorrow, not the next day, but eventually a big gain is made. Don't look for the big, quick improvement. Seek small improvements one day at a time. That's the only way it happens—and when it happens, it lasts."

The journey matters, not the destination. The process, not the outcome. If you can focus on getting a little bit better each day, through your practice and your training, then after 365 days you'll be a lot better. And then the trophies, titles, and championships will follow.

I now say that confidence isn't believing you will win all of the time. That's artificial optimism. Confidence is believing you'll do the best you can. The former you can't control; the latter you can. I believe it's a more realistic viewpoint, and for me a more successful one.

Fast forward four years. It's the Eastern Michigan open, first tournament of my third year in college. The score is tied 2-2 in overtime. The last 7 ½ minutes have been nothing but intense scrambles. The battle has left me exhausted and with :30 seconds left I can barely feel my legs. My opponent shoots a double leg and drives me towards my back, but I refuse to give this up. I do my funky Pennsylvania roll, where I reach for his ankles and pull them over top of me, and get back to my base. I lift him up and scramble with everything I have left to get the winning takedown. As I walk off of the mat my teammates congratulate me in awe for beating a two-time state champ. I guess it wasn't expected that I would. But I didn't know that.

Looking back to my wrestling days, I performed best when I didn't worry about the results, or if I were ready or not, or about letting myself or others down. It was when I just had fun and gave it everything I had that my performance excelled. It took me many years to get this. Thankfully, I did.

Life is not about you. The winning mindset isn't just for your benefit. There are people out there who need you. Believe that you'll be the best you can and you will… For them.

I love you, son. I believe in you. Now believe you're a champion today. It's an absolute game-changer.

FIND THE WHY

—

The femur is not a good bone to break. It's one of the largest and strongest bones in the body. According to most doctors it's not a bone that likes to heal properly.

So we shrieked when we found out that our good friend Tricia broke her right one at our sprint obstacle race, called the Hitman Challenge. The Hitman is a series of eleven tough man/woman obstacles including army crawls, tractor tire flips, sandbag carries, monkey bars, an eight-foot Big Daddy wall, plus more. The event was a hit. There were so many highs. But this unfortunate injury is the only thing that stuck in my mind for days.

Tricia slipped off the last monkey bar and landed on her right hip. She played off her agony cool, but we didn't. Just moments earlier she explained that she didn't want to go a second round, but we all encouraged her to. "Come on Tricia, you can do it. You're Hardcore!" So after the ambulance pulled away, the guilt set in.

Tricia is all but a buck and some change on the scale. She's a tiny tike, but her heart is fierce. When I saw her sense of humor shine even while lying immobile on the hospital bed, I started realizing that something magical was about to happen. Over the next few weeks many of us would see that magic unfold.

Tricia exemplifies what I call an awakening attitude. She accepted her situation and moved full force to recovery. She understood that this didn't just happen to her, but for her to inspire others. Her setback turned into another's catapult.

Nietzsche once said that, "That which doesn't kill you makes you stronger." I love this quote. It means if you're not dead then you have something to live for. There's a reason for your existence. There's no mountain too high, no pit too deep, no wall too solid, no struggle too tough that you can't endure.

When life hits you hard, "TRIPLE AAA" comes to the rescue. It's an acronym I made up one day when thinking about how to push through struggles.

1. AWARENESS

First you have to be aware of what's going on. What happened? This isn't just a menial observation, but a full grasp, consciousness, comprehension of the magnitude, effect, and implication of the situation.

2. ACCEPTANCE

Next is accepting your current situation. You get it. Everything happens for a reason. It is what it is, good, bad, or indifferent; nothing is going to change. God told you he has plans for you, *"plans for welfare and not for evil, to give you a future and hope"* (Jeremiah 29:11). And now it's time to figure out what those plans are.

3. AWAKENING

Then comes the "and then some." So what are you going to do about it? Are you going to let it make you or break you? Shut down and you'll miss an opportunity to let your suffering serve something greater. Let out the giant within and you can use your situation to positively impact as many people as you can.

Let's put things into perspective. When you think life is difficult, think about holocaust survivors like Elie Wiesel. In his book, *Night*, he recounts his experience as a prisoner in concentration camps. As a teenager his family was ripped from their home. They were separated. His mother and sister presumably killed in the gas chambers. His father was later beaten to death by SS soldiers.

Read some of these snippets I highlighted from his book:

> "All Jews, outside! Hurry!" They were followed by Jewish
> police, who, their voices breaking, told us: "The time has
> come...you must leave all this..." The Hungarian police
> used their rifle butts, their clubs to indiscriminately strike
> old men and women, children and cripples.
>
> I no longer felt anything except the lashes of the whip.
> "One!...Two!..." he was counting. He took his time between
> lashes. Only the first really hurt. I heard him count:" Ten...
> eleven!.." His voice was calm and reached me as through
> a thick wall. "Twenty-three..." Two more, I thought, half
> unconscious. The Kapo was waiting. "Twenty-four...twenty-
> five!" It was over. I had not realized it, but I had fainted.
>
> "Meir, my little Meir! Don't you recognize me...You're
> killing your father...I have bread...for you too...for you
> too..." He collapsed. But his fist was still clutching a small
> crust. He wanted to raise it to his mouth. But the other
> threw himself on him. The old man mumbled something,
> groaned, and died. Nobody cared. His son searched him,
> took the crust of bread, and began to devour it.

Elie's book hit me right when I needed to hear it. I read it at a pivotal time
in my life, and it gave me an entirely different outlook; one of gratitude
and appreciation. Who am I to complain? Do I really think I have struggles? It was time to think again.

Imagine sitting in your house one day. Soldiers show up at your door
and physically remove you and your family. No possessions. No comfortable clothes. No last minute goodbyes. They force you into a truckload
full of your neighbors. This is the last time you'll spend with your mom
and sister. You and your dad will suffer side by side for the next year and
eventually he'll die too. You'll barely make it out alive. Then imagine trying to find the WHY from it all.

An estimated 11 million people died during the Holocaust during
World War II. Not many of those who survived were able to do so with

an awakening attitude. All were aware. I'm sure most accepted. But not many were able to see their suffering as worthy to inspire. Elie awakened. And he won a Nobel Peace Prize for doing so.

Thankfully Tricia shared the same mindset. When life gave Tricia lemons, she enjoyed them. Tricia could have been bitter and sour if she tasted her situation like everyone else. But she chose to focus on the little things that matter, like spending the extra downtime with her family, strengthening bonds with her friends during house visits and trips to rehab, and becoming an inspirational leader with the geriatric crowd. I love the story she told of an elderly lady she met at rehab who didn't think she could do an exercise like Tricia did. Tricia encouraged her to try harder and believe in herself. The next week the elderly lady found Tricia and said, "I did it, you were right, I was able to!"

When pain kicked up a notch, she laughed more to make her stronger. It's no wonder she was voted class CLOWN in high school. Tricia has fun with everything. She sent videos of her grocery store wheelchair races; she made workout videos of her ankle stretches; she did tricks with her cane. She used her sense of humor to pull her through the tough ruts. And it wasn't always easy. "I will admit it has been hard. Sometimes I was in pain during and after PT, but I always cracked a joke just to shrug it off. I didn't want anyone to see me struggling. I think the PT guys Deryl and Darin think I am slap happy, HAHA." Happiness is a choice; she chose to keep a smile on her face.

In order to get her body right, she knew she had to get her mind there first. She was going to recover and nothing was going to stop her. Her body followed along with the plan. "Nobody can bring me down. I can only go up or forward. I am going to rock the house when I get back to Fit Me Up! Look out! I will be even more powerful...even if it takes a while!" With a mindset like this, there's no way you'll lose when life knocks you down, makes you hit walls, or slips your grip off of monkey bars.

Struggles will break you if you let them. Tricia didn't. She saw the good that could come from a travesty. She saw the growth that could come from a loss. She permitted the strength that could come from a weakness. And because of it, she let a lot of people into her world to sense the magic that comes from doing so.

Tricia would never want her situation to be related to that of Elie Weisel's. Their stories aren't comparable, but their ability to find their WHY is. Struggles may differ in degree, but generally our response to them is the same. Both of these individuals demonstrate an awakening one.

I end with what Elie Weisel said at the conclusion of his Nobel Prize acceptance speech, "We know that every moment is a moment of grace, every hour an offering; not to share them would mean to betray them. Our lives no longer belong to us alone; they belong to all those who need us desperately."

Life is not about you. Hopefully you never have to break your femur to prove that.

I love you, son. I believe in you. Now find your WHY today. It's an absolute game-changer.

THE CHAMPION ATTITUDE

—

Life is all about attitude. My mom has a great one. The short 5'1" full-blooded Italian woman grew up in a small Italian community in Youngstown, Ohio called Brier Hill. There she grew up with thousands of other Italians who labored in the steel mills just down the hill. The culture immersed her with the three F's that all Italians enjoy: food, faith, and family.

Carmela then married my full-blooded Italian father in 1976. They settled in a nine hundred square feet, three-room house just outside of Youngstown where they raised their full-blooded Italian family of six for the next thirty-five years.

We never had much, but according to my mom we were rich. For many years my dad raised us on minimum wage. Hand-me downs clothed us. Used cars drove us. Food stamps fed us. From others' viewpoint we looked poor. We had family though. We had everything.

A small house—great, it kept the family close. The car breaks down again—good, makes you appreciate it when it works. Pasta again—at least we have food. An apple a day keeps the doctor away? No, hugs do. The amount of money in your bank makes you wealthy—no, the amount of kisses your mom gives you makes you healthy.

While others would have surely stressed over rough times, my mother stressed the importance of looking at the bright side. It makes me fully grasp the concept that you can't always control what happens to you in life, but you can always control your reaction to it.

People can't get you angry unless you let them. Road blocks can't stop you unless you don't go around them. Life doesn't stink unless you don't ask for more. It reminds me of these great lines from a poet: (taken from Napolean Hill's "*Think and Grow Rich.*")

"I bargained with Life for a penny,
And Life would pay no more,
However I begged at evening
When I counted my scanty store.
For Life is a just employer,
He gives you what you ask,
But once you have set the wages,
Why, you must bear the task.
I worked for a menial's hire,
Only to learn dismayed,
That any wage I had asked of Life,
Life would have willingly paid."

Life will give you what you want. You just have to ask for it.

Just ask Erik Weihenmayer. He climbed to the summit of the world's highest peak-Mt. Everest on May 25, 2001. Seven years later in 2008, he would stand on top of Carstensz Pyramid in Australia to complete his quest to climb the seven summits-the highest peak on every continent-a true feat for any human being. What makes this story even more significant is Weihenmayer accomplished this all while being BLIND.

Vision—you have to have a positive one. Erik could have let the lack of his sight stop him. He could have listened to others. But he chose to see his situation differently, and now he's earning what he asks of Life. In order to see it differently you have to talk to yourself differently. Listen to this wise story a mentor once told:

"An old Cherokee told his grandson, "My son, there is a battle between two wolves inside us all. One is Evil. It is anger, jealousy, greed, resentment, inferiority, lies and ego. The other is Good. It is joy, peace, love, hope, humility, kindness, empathy, & truth." The boy thought about it, and asked, "Grandfather, which wolf wins?" The old man quietly replied, "The one you feed."

What you plant into your head you will harvest. Plant negative thoughts and negative actions will grow. Plant positive thoughts and positive actions will grow. *"For as he thinketh within himself, so is he* (Prov 23:7)."

There's an interesting phenomenon among the Italian culture. They eat a lot. They are not the most in-shape-people group (I know this is a generalization, but it's just my experience). Yet typical health complications are not a concern for them. In fact, a study was done in a small town called Roseto, Pennsylvania. It's the introduction to Malcom Gladwell's book, Outliers. The people of Roseto amazed doctors with their health. Compared to most Americans, this Italian community has a low occurrence of heart disease. And although they were obese, they lived long lives.

After analyzing the data, the doctors could only attribute it to one thing, their social structure. The people of Roseto enjoyed simplicity. They valued family, in many cases with multiple generations living under one roof. They stopped to talk to neighbors. Their civic organizations were strong. Their churches were calm. Their physicality might have been equivalent to most Americans, but their attitudes were vastly different. And so was their health.

What you see is what you get. In general, Italians see life as pleasurable, plentiful, and bountiful. La vita e bella (life is beautiful), and that's what they get. Not the stress, nor the complications that come with it, as most people do.

My mom doesn't think she gave me much. But I nominate her for coach of the year. She instilled in me the attitude of a champion. In my opinion, she gave me everything.

Life is not about you. Having a great attitude doesn't just affect you. It's contagious to all those around you.

I love you, son. I believe in you. Now have the attitude of a champion today. It's an absolute game-changer.

CHOOSE YOUR INSANITY

One of my favorite movies to watch is One Who Flew Over the Cuck-oo's Nest. It's a classic. I remember watching it with my parents as a high schooler, but I loved it more because of the funny crazy people and big Chief Wahoo. It wasn't until I watched it again in college did I appreciate the value behind the message.

Jack Nicholson plays a jail bird who decides to pretend he has a mental illness so he can be transferred to a mental hospital. There he will try to develop an escape plan. He's admitted into a particular group with some mentally ill patients. He observes the strict and rigid staff members who treat you like you're crazy. Jack Nicholson wants to escape. He's frustrated because no one else wants to. Then in a group therapy session one day he realizes that each patient actually CHOOSES to be there.

What a metaphor for life. So many people choose to imprison themselves. They let stress take over. Worry becomes their normal. Others habitually make them angry. They act like it's not in their control, and as a result, they voluntarily admit themselves into their own asylum. Which affirms this quote: *"Death is more universal than life; everyone dies but not everyone lives."*–Alan Sachs

Living comes down to the power of choice. It's one of the greatest gifts God ever gave us. You choose to go through the motions or create it. You can stand on the sidelines or get in the game. You can ask what happened, watch what happens, or make things happen. You choose to be insane in the brain or insane in His name.

Insane in the brain

When you're insane in the brain, you're negative. Complain a lot. Refuse to look at the bright side. Freeze before you even take that first step.

Insane in His name

When you're insane in God's name, you'll take risks, you'll be courageous, you'll be positive. You'll do what Philippians 4:8 says and *"Fix your thoughts on what is true, and honorable, and right, and pure, and lovely, and admirable. Think about things that are excellent and worthy of praise."* (NLT) You'll listen to what Romans 12:2 says and *"Do not conform to the pattern of this world, but be transformed by the renewing of your mind."*

And then the juices get flowing. The energy doesn't stop. You'll look crazy. Paul did when he was beaten and stoned and left for dead outside the city of Lystra, but then got back up and re-entered to continue spreading the good news of the Gospel (Acts 14:8-20). He looked crazy; but he felt alive.

You'll look crazy when you tell your friends that instead of going out on a Friday night, you're going to church to hang out with your life group.

But the Good Samaritan did too, when he stopped to help the Jewish man who was left for dead on the side of the road (Luke 10:25-37). Samaritans didn't associate with Jews back then. It was severely frowned upon. But he didn't care. He stopped. And looked weird.....but felt alive.

You'll look nuts when you do what God wants and think what He thinks. I don't know about you, but this is the asylum where I want to be. Because guess what? It's where the ultimate Physician does His residency. This is where He heals. This is where you get medicine that you can't get over the counter.

Life is not about you. The power of choice is ultimately what your mental state comes down to. You're going to have to decide what type of INSANITY you want to live. Eventually, you'll need to help a group of prisoners escape from their asylum.

I love you, son. I believe in you. Now get out there and be insane in His name today. It's an absolute game-changer.

FEAR HAPPENS, GET OVER IT

"Courage is not the absence of fear. It's being scared as heck and still doing it anyways." — *Unkown*

Standing on the platform three stories up, I freeze. I know that's what I'll do when I hit in the ice cold water below. There's no turning back though. At least fifteen mudders line up the climbing wall behind me. It's either jump into the water or irritate a lot of people by making them climb back down. I don't like heights. I don't like cold water. At my attempt to launch, fear grips me, and I retract my first step.

I think of Joshua. Perhaps he hesitated too. God called him to take his army across the Jordan River into the city of Jericho. To get to the Promised Land they had to cross through it. At ten square miles this fortress seemed unconquerable. No one came out and no one went in (Joshua 6:1). From human glance, Joshua's army didn't stand a chance against Jericho's highly equipped thousands. But in God's eyes, the job was already done. Joshua just had to enter the city with his herd of believers and follow his commands. One being, "Be strong and courageous." He must have wanted him to hear it because He repeated it three times in these verses. A command, not recommendation. He insists. He means it. God had plans for Joshua and He wanted him to trust his lead.

Sometimes that's hard to do. Fear is debilitating. It's restricting. It can numb. Like when I'm standing in line at the shock therapy obstacle. It's the part of the race when you army-crawl through water while trying to avoid the hanging, worm-like cords above you. Touch them and they'll shock you. I believed it once I heard the jolts and screams from those in front of me. It was rather funny, but how was it going to feel? I wasn't fond of finding out.

The Tough Mudder is loaded with these mental challenges. Over twenty obstacles are spread over thirteen miles of muddy, hilly, terrain. Part endurance event, part hiking adventure, this Navy Seal-created course puts your mind to the test. Although physically it wasn't that demanding, it definitely wasn't your normal run in the park. Often you had to push yourself out of your comfort zone.

Like a good friend did to me in Nicaragua a few months earlier. We were down there on a mission trip with our youth group. Twenty teenagers, five adults, one mission—to serve those in need. We did a lot of good work, building a foundation for a new preschool, painting a church, and setting up vacation bible schools for a few barrios. But we also had fun.

One day we went zip lining. We traveled what seemed like forever up a steep mountain to the starting point. I didn't think it was mandatory for everyone. But after getting fitted for our head gear, gloves, and harnesses, I realized Pastor Tom MacMillan, my friend and leader of the trip, didn't really give me an option.

Irritated, frustrated, and full of anxiety about the coercion, I approached the first zip line. Tom and the crew encouraged me. If the kids were doing it, I had to man up and do it too. Somehow I just walked to the contraption, let the instructor hook me up, and let myself go. It was frightening, and so were the next eleven of them, but I got over it.

Looking back, I knew Tom knew what he was doing. He knew I was scared of heights, he heard my comments on the trip up, but he saw an opportunity for growth. He gave me a nudge and I'm not sure I would have encountered this Tough Mudder race as composed as I did, had he not pushed me past a new threshold.

Overall, this was a great learning year about fear, and a perfect time to sit down and reflect. As I did, I came up with my Top Four Lessons about overcoming it:

1. FACE FEARS TO CONQUER THEM

We're not going to magically wake up one day fearless. Fear will be there. Our job is to figure out a way to plow through it. Entering the struggle and untangling yourself from it is when true growth happens. Eventually, fear will slowly release its grip, and taking risks each day becomes a conquest, because you know it's only going to transform you for the best. Climbing monkey bars over ice cold water, or crawling through water while being zapped, isn't necessarily something you look forward to. But the person that you'll become after you get through it is.

2. THE OUTCOME DOESN'T MATTER AS MUCH AS THE PROCESS DOES

It doesn't matter if you take a step and fall flat on your face. You'll get back up a better person, and you'll learn to take a different step next time. More often than not you can't predict what's going to happen or how it's going to happen. That's ok. Just enjoy the journey. Joshua was told to march around the city for seven days, quietly too, with only trumpets sounding on occasion. I can just imagine what was going through his head---how in the world is this going to result in a victory? But Joshua and his men didn't anticipate the end result. They stayed true to the call and followed suit day by day. And throughout the process they heard and saw things they never would have, like the parting of the Jordan River:
"Yet as soon as the priests who carried the ark reached the Jordan and their feet touched the water's edge, the water upstream stopped flowing. It piled up in a heap a great distance away, at a town called Adam in the vicinity of Zarethan, while the water flowing down to the sea of Arabah was completely cut off. So the people crossed over opposite Jericho." (Joshua 3:16)

3. ENLIST YOUR A-TEAM

You need support and camaraderie. You need someone to lift you up when you fall. You need someone to tap into you and unleash your true potential. Courageous people have mentors. Courageous people have teammates. "A chord of three strands is not easily broken." (Ecclesiastes 4:12)

At the Tough Mudder I came to many obstacles and said "I think I'll just skip this one!" If I were by myself, I'm sure I would have. But I was with an awesome team. We really didn't give each other an option. We just did it. We lined up, we encouraged each other, and we knew we were in this together.

4. THE ONLY THING HOLDING YOU BACK IS YOU

Imagine if Joshua would have held himself back. He wouldn't have done the unthinkable or brought his people the invaluable—a total reliance on God. Victory did happen. *"By faith the walls of Jericho fell, after the people had marched around them for seven days."* (Hebrews 11:30).

You wake up every day with a choice of who you want to be. Why do you do what you do, or don't do what you want to do? You have to play Big in life to Be Big. Take risks. You may be working hard to overcome an addiction, to pursue a new career, or to be a better leader in your household. There are no excuses; people are waiting for you to take that next step. Whether you're scared or not, you need to take it.

On the next step I did end up jumping into the Water. Free falling thirty feet brought my stomach to my throat. I didn't know what it was going to feel like when I landed, I just trusted I would figure out a way to get out. The cold water was a shock, but before I went into shock I scrambled to the surface. It was scary to take that jump, but after getting back to my feet, I got over it. I had to. It was time to move on to the next obstacle. My teammates were waiting.

There will be many times in life when fear tries to stop you: your first wrestling match, the history speech you have to present in front of the entire class, the launch of your new business idea. First remember God's word, *"Be strong and courageous. Do not be terrified; do not be discouraged, for the Lord your God will be with you wherever you go."* (Joshua 1:9) He'll be with you every step, and he'll give you answers along the way. Second, remember it's really not about you. You'll learn something new along the way and your faith will be strengthened. And that's only going to help you become a better person, a stronger one, for all those who need you.

Life is not about you. Be strong and courageous. It will help get your followers to the Promised Land and your teammates across the last electric shock obstacle to the finish line, three and a half hours later.

I love you, son. I believe in you. Fear happens. Now get over it today. It's an absolute game-changer.

I USED TO BE

I used to spray paint bums.
I used to smash beer cans over my head.
I used to do whip-its.
I used to make out with girls without even knowing their name.
I used to watch porno.
I used to say the F-word in every sentence.
I used to be afraid of what people thought about me.
I used to be scared to try something new.
I used to never raise my hand first.
I used to buckle under pressure.
I used to dwell on my defeats.
I used to let others get me angry.
I used to feel inadequate because I didn't have money.
I used to be afraid to write this because of how you would think of me.
But then I got saved. I realized there was a way out and that the past
didn't dictate my future.
I realized my abilities weren't fixed.
My character wasn't permanent.
My personality could change.
My ego could alter.
My mindset could shift.
My heart could renew.
My weaknesses could make me stronger.
I didn't have to be that way.

I could choose a different life and become the man that I was meant to.
But it doesn't stop there.
This is spiritual warfare.
And to win it means I have to constantly be in it,
And I have to **HAVe iT** every single day.
Humility. Authenticity. Vulnerability. Transparency. Four game-changing words I used to not even be able to pronounce. Now I try to experience them every single day. They keep me right where I need to be, in a place to be molded, shaped, and constantly reconfigured as I try to figure this all out.

Humility

It's about knowing you can always learn, grow, and get better. It's a hard place to be. Once you think you're there, you're not. But it may be the state of being that captures God's gaze the most—because it repels the deadliest of sins—PRIDE.

How do you stay there? You constantly check yourself and allow yourself to get checked by others. Ask yourself and others what you're doing wrong and how you can get better. *"God opposes the proud but shows favor to the humble."* (James 4:6 NIV)

Authenticity

Be the real you, all the time, and everywhere. You want people to look at you and say what you see is what you get. There's no sugar coating, no faking who you are to fit in or look better, no worrying about the response by others. If you feel it needs to be said, speak the truth in love and say it. It doesn't matter if people judge you, or think you're weird, or get offended. God knows where your heart is. *"The LORD does not look at the things people look at. People look at the outward appearance, but the LORD looks at the heart."* (1 Sam 16:7)

Vulnerability

Get uncomfortable, be unsafe, open yourself up—you never know where it will take you. Some of the hardest things to hear are what caused me to change the most.

It's ok to not be fully prepared. Being 100% prepared means you'll rely on yourself; to not, means you'll rely on God. Stay there.

Transparency

Let people see through you. It doesn't mean you're not protected. You can still have a shield up, just a glass one so people can see who's behind it. People respect it when you're open and honest. It may feel like a temporary release of power, but it will result in so much more.

The truth will set you and others free. Most of the time it's not about you; it's more about what others can gain from it. I can't tell you how many times I have been convicted by brothers who have been transparent and shared vices, struggles, and wounds with me.

To **HAVe iT** everyday helps us get closer and closer to being more like Jesus. It takes us out of the complacent stage that Paul talks about in Romans 7:15…*"That which I want to do, I do not do. And that which I hate to do is exactly what I do."*

Being saved is one thing. Acting saved is a whole different ball game.

> We tend to lean on the fact that acts alone
> can't bring us salvation,
> But we forget the fact that gratitude for his Grace alone
> should drive us to pursue constant sanctification.
> Mistakes were erased—
> doesn't mean we keep making them.
> Sins were forgiven—now it's time to start replacing them.
> Excuses can't be tolerated.
> Lukewarmness must be annihilated.

Life is not about you. Being Christ isn't easy. As a matter of fact, it's not possible. But it doesn't mean we don't strive for it anyways. That's actually all that he asks for.

I love you, son. I believe in you. Now let's **HAVe iT** today. It's an absolute game-changer.

ELEVATE GOD, NOT YOURSELF

—

He was strong and mighty. He defeated an entire army by himself. He tore a lion in half with his bare hands. He captured my attention.

Samson is an iconic biblical figure. At first glance, he's what every man wants to be. He is ripped and chiseled. He could take out thousands of soldiers with only his fists. The ladies loved him. He had power, brawn, and might. But then you read about him and realize he isn't as great as he seems. He slaughtered roughly one thousand people with the jawbone of a donkey, he took advantage of women, and he sought revenge on his opponents, the Philistines, by setting the tails of three hundred foxes ablaze.

Samson was chosen by God before he was born. God gave him incredible superhuman strength and potential to do His work. Unfortunately, it wasn't long before he used it for his own glory instead. Despite knowing God's plans, he lived a selfish life, fulfilling his own desires, and took advantage of the gifts that he received.

Even though murder isn't on most people's rap sheets, we can relate Samson's life to the way many live today. Often, people build a platform for themselves with intentions of stocking it with everything they can in life. In all fairness, they've been somewhat misled. Books tell them it's about money and only money. Seminars promote climbing the corporate ladder as a means to happiness. Motivational speakers entice by promising that luxuries, cars, houses, and vacations are within reach, as if they were essentials. Because of our skewed perceptions, we think they are.

Success has been most inappropriately defined. For you I will redefine it.

Success is not about:

The amount of money in your bank account.

How many trophies you win.

The titles next to your name.

The luxury cars that you drive.

The brand-name clothes you wear.

The corporate ladders you climbed.

Success is about:

Being completely fulfilled with your life's work.

Discovering and using your gifts and abilities.

Finding and following your true calling.

Lying in bed at night fully content with how you lived your day,
 and waking up completely fired up to do it again.

On your quest for success, remember these two things:

1. BUILDING A PLATFORM FOR YOURSELF WON'T GET YOU ANY HIGHER

Just ask the Babylonians. Many years after Noah's ark survived the flood that wiped out humankind, humans began rebuilding. The population grew and so did their talents. They became smart and ambitious and decided it was time to make a name for themselves. Their goal: to build a tower high enough to reach heaven for all to recognize who they were. Read the short story below from Genesis 11: 1 (The MSG):

> At one time, the whole Earth spoke the same language. It so happened that as they moved out of the east, they came upon a plain in the land of Shinar and settled down.
>
> They said to one another, "Come, let's make bricks and fire them well." They used brick for stone and tar for mortar. Then they said, "Come, let's build ourselves a city and a tower that reaches Heaven. Let's make ourselves famous so we won't be scattered here and there across the Earth."
> GOD came down to look over the city and the tower those people had built.
>
> GOD took one look and said, "One people, one language;

why, this is only a first step. No telling what they'll come up with next—they'll stop at nothing! Come, we'll go down and garble their speech so they won't understand each other." Then GOD scattered them from there all over the world. And they had to quit building the city. That's how it came to be called Babel, because there GOD turned their language into "babble." From there GOD scattered them all over the world.

Striving to build a platform for your own recognition may fill you, but it doesn't fulfill you. It may get you platinum records, but it doesn't earn you an eternal one. It may get you high, but it doesn't get you far, especially in God's kingdom.

2. ELEVATE YOURSELF TO ELEVATE GOD

Not too long ago I had the opportunity to break a world record for the most Aztec pushups in one minute. The Aztec pushup is an acrobatic pushup in which you explode off the floor from a pushup, tap your toes with your hands, then land into a pushup again and execute another rep before face planting into the floor. The previous record was 31. I was able to do 36. I'm still waiting to see if the Guinness Book of World Records has accepted it yet. But, earning a spot in the record book was not the point. I didn't do this challenge to bring attention to me, or to earn bragging rights. I did it as an example for others to not just talk about goals, but to work hard to achieve them. And in the process, to bring all glory to God. Sometimes you need to capture people's attention by elevating yourself to a new and extreme stature. And then when their gaze is on you, you can direct it to the One who makes everything possible.

Samson does eventually redeem himself though, and I gain respect for him again. The last act before he dies is one of surrendering to God. The Philistines have finally captured him. They gouge out his eyes. They mock and harass him. They chain him and put him in prison. Then they bring him to the pillars in the town center for everyone to see. "Ha ha, nanner nanner, boo boo, you can't move," I imagine them saying. Samson digs deep one last time. Although now blind, with God's vision he sees.

"Sovereign Lord, remember me. Please, God, strengthen me just once more, and let me with one blow get revenge on the Philistines for my two eyes. Then Samson reached toward the two central pillars on which the temple stood. Bracing himself against them, his right hand on the one and his left hand on the other, Samson said, "Let me die with the Philistines! Then he pushed with all his might, and down came the temple on the rulers and all the people in it." And God uses him to kill the Philistines and deliver his people, the Israelites. (Judges 16:28-30)

Notice, it wasn't until Samson lost his life that he gained one. It wasn't until he decreased that God increased. It wasn't until he sank, that God was elevated.

Life is not about you. When you elevate God, you don't have to worry about elevating yourself. He'll take care of that for you.

I love you, son. I believe in you. Now get out there and elevate God today. It's an absolute game-changer.

FAILURE DOESN'T HAPPEN AS LONG AS YOU'RE TRYING

You will mess up.

The prodigal son did. He left his home with hopes for a better one. Young and naive, he thought the grass was greener elsewhere. A simple life on the farm wasn't as appealing as a wild life in the city. With a plan intact, he requested his share of his family's estate. His father granted this outrageous demand. *"Not long after that, the younger son got together all he had, set off for a distant country and there squandered his wealth in wild living."* (Parable found in Luke 15:11-32)

The prodigal son soon learned that the high life wasn't such a rosy adventure. When his money was gone, he would work as a servant feeding pigs while left with nothing to feed himself. Eventually he comes back to his senses and wants to come back to his family. But he's worried. He royally screwed up, and he knows it. Listen to his self-talk, *"I will set out and go back to my father and say to him: Father, I have sinned against heaven and against you. I am no longer worthy to be called your son; make me like one of your hired servants."* (Luke 15:18-20)

Home is where his dad's heart is though. His dad welcomes him back with wide open arms, in celebratory fashion. People can't believe it. It's one of the greatest stories of a father's love. Jesus tells it as an example of God's unshakable love for us. God's love never stops flowing, and because it doesn't, my love for you never will either.

You will mess up and that is ok. I will still be here for you, supporting, coaching, and encouraging. Never hold back in life because of fear of disappointing me. As long as your heart is in the right place and you make decisions with the best of intentions, I will stay in your corner to cheer you on.

Your journey in life will not be easy though. Here are some thoughts to help you along your way:

1. EXPECT WALLS

I hit a wall at mile seven coming out of the Chicago Bears' football stadium. This was my third year participating in the Men's Health Urbanathlon, a race consisting of more than ten obstacles spread out over more than ten miles. I was sprinting as fast as I could to make the top twenty-five. As I left the stadium stairs, my body felt depleted and for an instant I almost felt defeated. But, I expected this to happen. I didn't know when. I didn't know exactly how it would feel. I just knew it was coming.

Walls happen in performance events and in life. Your job is to figure out how to overcome them. No one said life would be easy. Even Jesus said it would be hard: *"In the world you will have trouble."* (John 16:33) If you do not plan for difficulties, then when they arise they'll catch you off guard and make you feel defeated. I like to say "anticipate, and then participate." Anticipate that your body and mind will want to shut down after one mile of stadium stairs, and then participate in overcoming the next three and a half miles of obstacles to finish out the race at number 24.

2. THAT WHICH DOESN'T KILL YOU
ONLY MAKES YOU STRONGER

"More than that, we rejoice in our sufferings, knowing that suffering produces endurance." (Romans 5:3) Struggles and trials make you a stronger person when you focus on the positives of what you can gain from them. No matter the outcome, as long as you tried, you're going to learn, grow, and get better. Just put yourself out there and see what happens. You'll be surprised by who and what you find.

3. I LOVE WATCHING YOU WHEN YOU TRY

I just love watching you when you perform at your best. I love watching you when you play hard. I love watching you when you get back up after you get knocked down. Of course I would love to see you stand at the top of every podium, but my main concern will always be that you gave it everything you've got. If you do that, then you're a winner in my book, regardless of what the scoreboard says.

4. HARNESS YOUR STRENGTHS, DON'T DWELL ON YOUR WEAKNESSES

There is a new superhero in town. He cannot fly like superman, or demolish a building with his fist like the hulk, or scale walls like Spiderman, but he has no fear. He knows he'll use whatever skill he does have to be victorious over his enemy.

You will be great at so many things in life, but you will also be terrible at others. If you dwell on the things that you're not good at, you'll miss the opportunities to harness the talents, strengths, and abilities you have been given.

Be realistic and practical. If you're power is to fly — then fly. And if you can't smash buildings, don't spend your life striving to.

This doesn't mean you can't try to enhance your smashing abilities, but do not focus on them so much that you miss the opportunities to be a great flyer. Dwelling on your weaknesses will only immobilize you. Remember, a superhero doesn't learn to fly if he's too busy crying about his missing powers.

We are all gifted in different ways. Romans 12:8 says, *"If your gift is to encourage others, be encouraging. If it is giving, give generously. If God has given you leadership ability, take the responsibility seriously. And if you have a gift for showing kindness to others, do it gladly."*

5. CARE BUT DON'T CARE

I have found through my training experiences that the best athletes generally do not care. They are performers. They do what they know best and forget about the rest. They don't obsess about hitting a homerun beforehand. They don't dwell on a strike-out after. They show up at home plate, put their feet in the batter's box, and swing the best they can. I want you to care about exceeding your potential at each at-bat, but if you miss the ball, it is not the end of the world. Get back in and swing your hardest, and don't let the next pitch whiz right by you. If it does, try again.

When you read further into the prodigal son's story, you'll notice that not everyone was as welcoming as his father. His older brother was angry. He couldn't understand how his father could accept his younger brother's return so easily. The older brother says, *"Look! All these years I've been slaving for you and never disobeyed your orders. Yet you never gave me even a young goat so I could celebrate with my friends. But when this son of yours who has squandered your property with prostitutes comes home, you kill the fattened calf for him!'* (Luke 15:29-30)

"'My son,' the father said, 'you are always with me, and everything I have is yours. But we had to celebrate and be glad, because this brother of yours was dead and is alive again; he was lost and is found.'" (Luke 15:31-32)

Instead of prodigal, I call you the "Prodigy Son," Gio. You are so talented, mature, and advanced and I know you'll always land on solid ground, which means I'm not worried about you wandering off the beaten path. In fact, I'll probably encourage it. Sometimes you have to veer off to explore, discover, and become acquainted with who you are. It's on your search that you'll figure out where you came from and where you're going. So whatever dreams you may have, shoot for them. If you do get lost along your journey, have no worry. I know for a fact that you will eventually find yourself, and I want you to know that I will be waiting with wide open arms when you do.

Life is not about you. Don't let the fear of messing up prevent you from performing at your best. Making mistakes does not make you a failure. In my opinion, failure doesn't exist as long as you're trying.

I love you, son. I believe in you. Now get out there and try your hardest today. It's an absolute game-changer.

MY TWO CENTS ON MONEY

—

I will keep this chapter rather short and sweet. I don't want to—nor do I have the right to-try to cover the magnitude of this topic in one chapter. I have learned a lot about money the hard way though. As a result, I am entirely different with the way I handle it today.

I made a mess of my life during my second year in college. All of a sudden I found myself deep in credit card debt. For some reason credit card companies prey on college students. Even though you report no income, they love to give you something that requires you to have some. Eventually you have to pay it back, you know. For some reason I didn't realize that. They knew that, and they took advantage of my vulnerabilities and naivety. Although it only took one year to pile up eight thousand dollars in debt, it took me at least five years to get rid of it.

Money is a dangerous thing, especially when you don't have any. Your mind will play tricks on you, and you'll want what you can't have. It doesn't help to live in a country that has plenty.

We currently live in an extremely wealthy community. Just a block away are several blocks of million-dollar homes. I walked into one recently. It's decked out completely. The marble entryway floor is more expensive than my house. There are rooms that no one even uses. The playroom is something I could play in forever. Just when I think I need this, I remind myself it's just a big lie and a false high.

Material possessions may make you feel valuable on earth, but they'll never hold eternal value in heaven. When you die, God doesn't request that you pack up your Lexus and diamond rings and bring them with you. So although we use the accumulation of things to temporarily fill a void while we're living, they'll never permanently fulfill it. Eventually, no matter how much you have, you'll still come up empty. *"Whoever loves money never has money enough; whoever loves wealth is never satisfied with his income. This too is meaningless."* (Eccles. 5:10)

Money doesn't make you happy. Thankfully, your mom and I witnessed this firsthand. During our early twenties, we worked for a couple that had a lot of it. They brought in $65,000 a month at times. That was more than we made in two years combined. But this family was more miserable, toxic, and corrupt than we could handle. He embezzled money. She treated people like slaves. Their children were neglected. It was an eye-opening and convicting experience for us. We ran away from their rat race as fast as we could. They chased us away from ever wanting to chase money.

Money is complicated. Here's my two cents on it. Wait, let's add some interest. Make it ten cents.

WHEN YOU EARN IT:
1.Don't love it.
The love of money is the root of all evil. That's not just cliché, it's the truth (1 Tim. 6:10). People kill. Thieves steal. Wars are started. Marriages end. All because of people's infatuation with currency. Don't let it get the best of you. Change your heart toward money so you don't change the person you are in order to earn it.

2. Lead with your heart, the money will follow.
Entrepreneurs and business leaders would shriek if they knew our business strategy. We don't project numbers to hit each month, we project people. Our first and foremost goal is to impact as many lives as we can. We design our programs, culture, and financial structure around that. We focus on the people right in front of us and take care of them the best we can. The quality of our relationships with them matters. The quantity from there grows, and God makes the money flow. Granted, we don't make a lot of money, but we make a living and love every single second of what we do. That makes us richer than ever.

3. Make a budget.

Make a list of all your expenses and monthly income. Make note of your needs versus your wants. Ensure money is allocated to your needs first. Cut out the wants if you have to. Evaluate this budget regularly to be on top of what's coming in and where it's all going.

WHEN YOU SPEND IT:
4. Live below your means.

Just because you earn a certain amount of money doesn't mean you have to spend it all. Your basic needs outlined in your budget are not that many; food, shelter, clothing, insurance, utilities, supplies, etc. Be a minimalist and stick to the bare minimum. This doesn't mean that you can't have things or purchase nonessentials every once in a while. But it shouldn't be a regular thing, and it should be within reason. Go out to eat if it doesn't malnourish your surplus. Buy that extra outfit if it fits into your expense column comfortably. Purchase a house when you can easily live with its mortgage. Exceptions will happen, but try to keep them to exceptions.

5. You do have enough.

Just when you think you don't have enough, I want you to remember that some kids don't have food. Every year millions of kids die each year of starvation. I want you to remember that some kids live in landfills. I saw this first-hand on a mission trip in Nicaragua. We walked through mountains of trash and found families living and eating among them. You have running water. You have warm shelter. You have clothes on your back. Some kids minutes down the road from you live in a trailer park with a deadbeat dad smoking marijuana in the living room. They sleep on a bare mattress in a bare room in their bare skin in only a diaper. I saw this firsthand too. You are wealthier than 75% of the world's population just from making more than a few dollars a day. Living in the U.S. with a low income may make you feel like you're scraping, but compared to the rest of the world, you're raking.

6. Don't use money you don't have.

You should avoid credit cards and loans at all costs. Use a credit card with a small $250 balance as a way to build credit. Purchase items with it, then immediately pay it off. Don't apply for student loans if you don't need them. If you do, then only take out what you need.

WHEN YOU SAVE IT:
7. Find a financial coach.

You could figure out the best way to invest and save your money, but it takes a lot of time to figure it out. If it's not your full-time job, you may not have time to. There are so many options of funds, investment and retirement accounts, long-term insurance options, and stocks (I'm still clueless), leaving you confused about which direction to take. Not to mention the countless scams and get-rich-quick schemes that could steer somebody wrong.

Chances are you'll have friends or family members who handle finances for a living. Hire them. It costs pennies on the dollar to utilize their services and they'll save you hundreds of dollars and headaches from messing up on your own. Don't be a hero and let your bank account drop to zero. Find a money coach you trust and trust that they'll make you money. *"Of what use is money in the hand of a fool, since he has no desire to get wisdom?"* (Proverbs 17:16)

8. Start with these three accounts

1. Liquid account of at least three months of your expense needs. This is a basic savings account that you can access at any time without penalties and fees. If something were to happen and you couldn't work, you would want to be covered for a few months until you got back on your feet again.

2. Life insurance: Sometimes I'm proud that I'm worth more dead than I am alive. If I were ever taken early, I know you guys will be taken care of. I typically can't stand paying for insurance policies because you may rarely, if ever, use them. But of all the types, this is in my opinion the most important. After all, death is universal. Eventually it will be used.

3. Long-term retirement account: This is generally in the form of a 401k or a Roth IRA. Put something, no matter how big or small, away every month. It will add up fast. We will help you get this started at an

early age so you have a much better head start than we did. *"Dishonest money dwindles away, but he who gathers money little by little makes it grow."* (Proverbs 13:11)

WHEN YOU SHARE IT:
9. Tithe

A tithe is sharing a tenth part of your income to support the church. Technically when you tithe you're not sharing anything. You're giving back a portion of what God has shared with you. It's His money, and he only asks for 10% of it back. You should pay your church first even if not the full percentage. I do have somewhat of a different take on the tithing concept, which I'll explain in a second. What I do know for certain is you want to get to a point where your heart is in the right place. Be glad to give. *"Each one must give as he has decided in his heart, not reluctantly or under compulsion, for God loves a cheerful giver."* (2 Corinthians 9:7)

10. Give back to others

Your mom and I give away a lot of money. We give to individuals and organizations, we organize and financially sponsor charity events, we RAK (random act of kindness) people regularly, we sponsor two children in other countries. We see the value in it and we absolutely love doing it. We also tend to see this as counting as part of our tithe. After all, God said people are his church, he didn't say a building was. Now the church runs only because of its parishioners monetarily supporting it. It's a must, you have to pay them for their services, the same way our clients have to pay for memberships to keep our gym lights on. I'm just saying don't forget there's a body of people outside your church walls that God asks you to provide for too. And I'm not saying I'm right about all this, I'm just saying that's where I'm at right now. *"Give, and it will be given to you. Good measure, pressed down, shaken together, running over, will be put into your lap. For with the measure you use it will be measured back to you."* (Luke 6:38)

Oops, I didn't keep this chapter short after all. But you know what— your life is short. So you need this information to ensure you spend it wisely and your money too. Even though I don't make a lot of dollars, hopefully to you I make some sense.

Life is not about you. It's ok to have money but don't let it have you. You don't have time to let financial stress hold you down when you need to be free and ready to lift others up.

I love you, son. I believe in you. Now be a good steward of God's money today. It's an absolute game-changer.

TRIP TO MATTERS MOUNTAIN

I was once voted "best trainer in the area". . . No I wasn't. But I have been called "prince charming of a lifetime," by my wife. The "most gentle-hearted young man" by my mom. The "coolest guy in da whole world" by you. Perhaps I should place these titles on my website.

Accolades. Credentials. Highlights. We love putting them by our name. But what do they really mean anyway?

I have to watch that I don't cross the line. I used to want them by my name. Industry leaders who had theirs made me jealous. "The best of this," "the expert of that," "world renowned when it comes to those." But I could easily go from wanting to be the best at my job, to losing a part of myself in the process. Balance can be a struggle. Priorities must constantly be straight.

I wrote this poem about the struggle that we as men deal with—the struggle to matter.

The Trip to Matters Mountain
The man grabbed his belongings,
kissed his son and wife and headed out the door.
"Honey, I'm heading to Matters Mountain,
I'll return as so much more."
It was his day to get to the top.
The view was so much better from there.
Once you made it, others looked up to you.
You mattered. You stole stares.

Perseverance must be mustered though,
Through three challenges that weren't much fun.
He's completed two before and today was ready,
To finish the last one.
First he must walk fastest
through Loserville and Nothingtown,
Forward, sideways, up and down.
No problem—he passed easily,
And earned "Best walker in each town."
Next challenge was a trek through
a fierce and determined crowd,
Pushing and shoving, elbows and trips,
voices screaming loud.
With no way to go through or under,
he couldn't be the same.
So over he went and earned the title
"Expert crowd surfer" by his name.
Finally came the mountain climb that took an entire day,
"I'm willing to do whatever it takes," was all he had to say
To the higher-ups of Matters Mountain as they reached out and
said hello,
"Now come with us and enjoy the view of all of those below!"
At the honorary dinner he received
his last distinguished brand,
"The most mattered man in the world"
will now attract him lots of fans.
He may have earned his titles and a chance to give a toast,
But on his quest to Matters Mountain he left behind what mat-
tered most.

I don't believe the quest for titles is a problem; it's the consumption that is. Not the chase, but the separation from what matters. For what good is it to be the best trainer in the world if my marriage is in shambles, the bond with my children weakens, and my house starts to crumble? *"What good is it to gain the whole world but lose my soul?"* (Mark 8:36)

I have to be careful I don't send the wrong message to kids. I love to pump them up and tell them to shoot for the stars, work harder than anyone out there, and give 110% effort to be the best at everything they do. But there's an addendum attached: make sure to channel that effort towards what matters first. We can't neglect the fine print. Put your calling before your titles; your purpose before your roles; your life prescriptions before your job descriptions. If you fail to invest in what matters most, then the rest doesn't matter at all.

Your mother and I revamped our priority list a few years ago when we started our business ministry Fit Me Up. God first, family second, work third, no matter what. It's been the best decision we ever made.

I'm not saying I wouldn't enjoy being recognized as the best trainer in the area. I'm not saying I won't continue climbing to the top of the mountain. But before anything I want these titles next to my name:
"The most loving husband."
"The ultimate dad."
"The best server of the One who gave him life."

> There's a secret route to the top of Matters Mountain
> not many people know,
> You have to take Peoples First Bridge
> and get to know others as you go.
> Shake hands, be cordial, and listen to
> the stories that they drop.
> Eventually your trip becomes easier,
> no speed walking, no crowd surfing,
> you'll be carried to the top.

I love you, son. I believe in you. Now be the best at focusing on what matters today. It's an absolute game-changer.

IT'S A WONDERFUL LIFE

—

In my favorite Christmas movie of all time, *It's A Wonderful Life*, Jimmy Stewart plays a small-town business and loan advisor named George Bailey. George is a fun, charismatic, driven young man with lots of ambition. He wants to travel the world, take life by the reins, and fulfill all his hopes and dreams. It's admirable. It's respectable. It's honorable. But as soon as he gets his break to set sail, life's storms delay his voyage.

First his father dies. George must take over in order for the family company to survive. His little brother Harry fails to take rightful responsibility for the family company as planned. He comes back from college with a wife and a different plan. As George and his newlywed, Mary, leave for their honeymoon, a panicked crowd huddles at his bank requesting their money. George gives all his honeymoon cash to them to satisfy their immediate needs. His trip, his getaway, was postponed again.

He just can't get out. He sacrifices his dreams for his townspeople for many years. Finally the breaking point comes. His uncle accidentally misplaced $8,000, causing the building and loan to hit rock bottom. People will be broke. Families will be stressed. George can't bear it anymore.

He takes to the bridge where he's about to take his life. At that point life has just become about him, and he doesn't see it as meaningful.

According to Suicide.org, suicide takes the lives of approximately 30,000 Americans each year. Nearly 750,000 attempted suicides take place each year in the United States. Extreme depression. Severe mental illness. Loss of hope. Inability to see another way. The feeling of inadequacy. Not feeling needed. Suicide is complex. There's not one single trigger that leads to it. But there is one common characteristic of suicide--it is selfish. You leave the people that love you. You leave the life that God gave you. You leave a world that needs you. At the moment one takes his or her life, life has become all about them.

Just in case you ever ponder whether or not life is worth it, here's a solid reminder of how great this gift is:

WHEN YOU THINK YOU DON'T HAVE MUCH
(Inspired by Og Mandino's *"The Greatest Miracle in the World."*)

When you think you don't have much, you realize you have the gift of movement, thanks to 600 muscles stitched in your body to allow you to squeeze your child tight, glide across the dance floor with your spouse, and run through the finish line of a screaming crowd.

When you think you don't have much, you realize you have the gift of strength, thanks to 250 bones jointed together that allow you to carry bags of groceries to a stranger's car, serve bowls of soup to the homeless, and bend to pick someone up when they get knocked down.

When you think you don't have much, you realize you have the gift of breath, thanks to an intricate respiratory system that performs 17,000 beats per day, blessing you to smell the soft, delicate skin of your baby, the fragrance of your wife's perfume, and the aroma of your mom's special homemade spaghetti sauce.

When you think you don't have much, you realize you have the gift of sight, thanks to 100 million receptors placed in your eyes to enable you to enjoy the magic of a leaf, a snowflake, a pond, an eagle, a child, a cloud, a star, a rose, a rainbow . . . and the look of love.

When you think you don' t have much, you realize you have the gift of thought, thanks to a brain with 13 billion nerve cells to help you file away every perception, every sound, every taste, every smell, every action you have experienced since the day of your birth.

When you think you don't have much, you realize you have the gift of sound thanks to 24,000 fibers in your ear to vibrate the wind in the trees, the tides on the rocks, the majesty of an opera, a robin's plea, children at play . . . and the words "I love you."

When you think you don't have much, you realize you have the gift of touch, thanks to 7 miles of nerve fiber running throughout your body that allow you to feel the warmth of a hug, the spark of a kiss, the soft hands of children when they hold yours, the accomplishment after a productive workout, and the gratification from a pat on the back.

When you think you don't have much, you realize you have a pulsating heart that beats about 36 million times per year thanks to oxygen being pumped hour after hour, day and night, while you're asleep or awake, through 60,000 miles of veins and arteries woven precisely throughout your masterpiece structure.

When you think you don't have much, you realize you have the gift of life; designed, constructed, and manufactured, simply for you to make it worth living.

When you think you don't have much, you realize you have everything.

Thankfully George did not take his life. As he is about to leap, Clarence, an angel sent to save him, jumps in the water to distract him. George jumps in to save him and instead of jumping to his death, he ends up jumping to his life.

Clarence shows George a glimpse of what life would be like if he were never born. His wife would be lonely. Mr. Potter, the crotchety rich man, would rule the town. His little brother would have died as a boy because George wasn't there to save him from the freezing lake. You may not see how your life fits into the equation. George didn't until Clarence took him out of it. Then he sees that nothing added up right. At this point life becomes more about the people who need George, and he sees life as a miracle.

In the last scene of the movie, George gets fired up for life. He runs home screaming at the top of his lungs in excitement. The Christmas tree is on. Music is playing. The spirit is back. He embraces his family with a new zest for life. Then the townspeople barge into his house and embrace him. While he was out contemplating his life, they collected all the money he needed to keep the business and loan company alive.

You may have to sacrifice your dreams as George did. Your bank account may close like George's did. You may think you're worth more dead than alive like George did.

But then you remember that life is not about you. God gave you a gift, enjoy it. Others think you're worthwhile, stay in it for them. Your life is a miracle intended to be cherished, appreciated, and honored. It is a wonderful life. Now choose to see it that way.

I love you, son. I believe in you. Remember how valuable you are today. It's an absolute game-changer.

LIVE LIKE YOU'RE DYING

———

"Teach us to number our days and recognize how few they are;
help us to spend them as we should." (Psalm 90:12)

———

That's what I'm doing as I write you this book. I imagine if I were taken in an instant. Who would teach you these lessons? Who would guide you? Who would answer your questions? Would you know how much I love you?

A compulsion takes over me to get this project done. I stare at you. You're playing in the living room, not knowing I'm paying attention. So much potential. So much character. So much innocence. Someday you'll grow up to experience a chaos you're not used to. People don't think like we do. They don't behave like we do. Cruelty. Disrespect. Ignorance. Drama. Challenges. Pressure. It is all part of growing up, but will you be able to handle it? The world is yours for your taking. Do you know that? Because tomorrow may be my last, I have to get my last word in. The thought of my absence is the motive behind my madness.

I think about dying a lot. It may sound morbid, but it's actually liberating. The more I think about it, the more I want to live my life to the fullest. It's when we realize that death is inevitable that we step up to do the impossible.

What if you found out tomorrow would be your last? I guarantee you would live differently today. You would pay attention to your loved ones around you more. You would speak with a different tone. The list would come out—you would assign your last meal, your last message, your last act. You would ensure you left this earth in a bang. But why wait until you're on a gurney?

It happened to me once. I was cruising down the hospital hall. Doctors all around me. My wife trailing behind me. They were pushing me as fast as they could to the operating room. It was a terrible feeling. They all knew I was dying, and so did I. I screamed at the top of my lungs for a second chance. Then I woke up.

What a miracle it is to do so. We should appreciate that daily. One day I was caught up and took for granted my awakening. Then Tracy sat in front of me. She has become a friend after becoming involved in our fitness classes. She's a survivor. Tracy has defeated breast cancer but explains that "terminal" means it will eventually come back and kill her. To make the situation worse, her husband was recently diagnosed with lung cancer. Its progressing fast, and they're aggressively taking every measure possible to stop it and to restart some normalcy in their lives for once.

Normal in Tracy's world consists of regular checkups and scans, coupled with constant anxiety over pending results. Research for promising trials. Trips across country to test a new drug. Visits to funerals of girlfriends who share the same journey but unfortunately lost their battle. Then a conversation that I couldn't imagine having; who will take care of the kids? Tracy and her husband draw up a plan because they have no choice but to plan for the worst.

When Tracy leaves, I take a deep breath. A breath that I don't take for granted. And I remind myself of this phrase: TOO BLESSED TO BE STRESSED.

Often we think we have something to complain about. To-do lists are waiting. Work isn't finished. Life isn't fair. Then you freeze and capture the moment. You're breathing, you're walking, and you're talking. Thousands of people aren't, because they didn't make it today. Before you miss living in the moment, count your blessings. You have way more than you think. You're too blessed to be stressed.

There are 1441 minutes in every day. How can you enjoy every single one of them?

I strongly recommend that you reflect on these five questions and deflect anything that tries to stop you from answering them and living them out:

1. What matters most to you?

Identify the most important things in your life. We live by God first, family and friends second, then work third. Then invest your time and efforts into each accordingly, in that order.

2. Does it really matter?

Before you sweat the small stuff, make sure you look at the bigger picture. Is it really worth your energy? Is it really a matter of life or death? If not, stop the mental chatter and focus on what matters. Negativity, stress, and anger over the little things, will keep you from tending to the most important things that you outlined above.

3. What do you want to accomplish before you die?

From serious to fun to attainable to seemingly impossible. A popular name for this list is the Bucket List. Create yours and start notching them off immediately.

4. How do you want to be remembered?

Lying in your coffin. People surround you at your funeral. The obituary is written. The eulogy is given. The memories are shared. What do you want people to say about you? What do you want them to learn from you? What do you want them to miss, now that you're gone?

5. If you could do anything you want with your life, money not being an issue, what would you do?

Dig down deep and find what this is, then go do it. No matter how difficult it may be, make it your vocation to pursue your passion. There's nothing better than waking from your dreams to live the life you dreamt of.

Today could be my last. I'm ok with that. I live with no regrets now. I do what God wants, when he wants, and how he wants. I cherish and live in each moment with you and our family. I do what I love and love what I do with fitness coaching and motivational speaking. And now my proudest accomplishment, this book for you.

Of course I want to live out the rest of my days with you. But like yours, my days are numbered. Only God can say how many I have left. The least I can do is everything I can to make the best of them. I scribe my life's work for you within these pages to do just that. I live today like it's my last.

Life is not about you. It's your turn now.

I love you, son. I believe in you. Live like you're dying today. It's an absolute game-changer.

CHASE SIMPLICITY

"Simplicity is the ultimate sophistication."
—Da Vinci

"Life is really simple, but we insist on making it complicated."
—Confucius

We chase a lot of things in this world.

We chase Prestige. Prosperity. Luxury.

We chase more money. More status. More gadgets. More stuff. And usually it leads to... More stress. More complications. More problems. As Biggie Smalls once said, *"The more money we come across, the more problems we see."* (Yes, I just busted out some 90's hip hop. Biggie Smalls was a very popular rapper during my high school years.)

Piling up our lives with material, nonessential, insignificant things of no eternal value tends to drive us further away from where God truly wants us to be. It buries us from reaching our true potential. It causes us to live a life that deep down inside we don't truly want to live.

It's not the possession of meaningless things that is the problem; but rather the chase, the pursuit, and the hunt for them that is.

I didn't always think like this. I spent much of my early college years racking up thousands of dollars in credit card debt. I thought I was supposed to have things, and without funds to acquire them, I reached out to four close friends to help: Chase, Best Buy, Gap, and Sears. I neglected the fact I would eventually be required to pay them back... with an enormous amount of interest tacked on too!

I was driven by materialism for only a short time in my life. For a long time, though, I felt pressure to go back to that mindset. I felt insecure and questioned my adequacy because according to the world's standards, I was supposed to want more.

Don't ever second-guess yourself.

When you're on a quest for things in life that are meaningful, your life is meaningful. When you're on a quest for things that aren't; it isn't.

You'll think I'm crazy, but I love the Amish. The Amish are a group of people who refuse to conform to the values and ideals of typical society. They ride in horse-drawn buggies instead of cars. They don't buy fancy clothes, and they don't use mainstream electricity or technology. Amish country is one of my favorite places to visit. Life there is quiet. It's wholesome. It's simple.

And simplicity, in my opinion, is the key to serenity.

Son, when you chase a life of simplicity, you'll reap the benefits of freedom, clarity, and wisdom.

You'll be going against the grain and trust me, people will look at you like you're a weirdo. In reality, according to the norm of society, you will be. Stay strong and keep taking the road less traveled.

Here are four laws of simplicity that I want you to remember:
1. LESS IS MORE
I don't know any aspects of life where this principle cannot be applied. So many times we try to get too technical or too savvy when all we have to do is revert to the basics. Take fitness training for example. People are always searching for the magic pill or the next high-tech gadget that will allow them to achieve optimal results with little to no work on their part. On the flip side, they may try to overdo it with insane and extreme, exhaustive workouts. Stay simple and be consistent. Get your body moving, breathe hard, strain your muscles, and eat healthy, earth-bred foods. Boom. The results will come. *"Often he who does too much does too little."*
–Italian Proverb

2. SLOW DOWN FAST

In our world, being busy translates to productivity which in turn looks like success. This "art" of life-cramming and multitasking prevents us from enjoying the everyday gifts that really matter, like time with those we love. A few months ago, our friend did something so admirable and unforgettable. With newborn twins and an active twenty month old he recognized that he didn't want anything to prevent him from cherishing his family time. So he demoted himself. He walked into his boss's office, requested a demotion, a position with fewer hours, fewer headaches and consequently less money. The decision wasn't easy but he knew in his heart it was right. He doesn't even know how blessed he'll be for putting his time with his family ahead of his pride, his status, and his fortune. That's a radical step in faith and will certainly result in an abundance of blessings.

3. REDUCE

Eliminate useless time wasters, insignificant toys & gadgets and material things. Down-size so you're not stressed about money. Free up your schedule so you have more time with family. Say "no" to things that aren't honorable to God. Nix negative thoughts, avoid gossip and unforgiving attitudes. Focus on climbing the ladder to God rather than the ladder to success. It will clear your mind, heart, and schedule to stay in-tune to what really matters.

4. LITTLE THINGS MAKE A BIG DIFFERENCE

You don't need anything extravagant to be extraordinary. Just be you. Reach out to people and invest in them. Jesus didn't have much, and He didn't use people with much either. Yet He's still changing millions of lives some two thousand years later. Little things go a long way and the greatest gift you could ever give is yourself. Give your ear, give your love, and give your time. That's all people ever need and want.

Gio, one of the best things your mom and I ever did was start chasing simplicity. There was a time when the pressure to obtain more and keep up with those around us did nothing more than accumulate unwanted stress and wreak havoc on our marriage.

Life is not about you. It takes a courageous person to be simple in today's complex world, but a funny thing happens when you are. You'll end up gaining more than you could ever imagine. And most importantly, you'll end up living the life you were meant to live.

I love you, son. I believe in you. Now chase simplicity today. It's an absolute game-changer.

FIND BALANCE

—

I love how God works. Sometimes when he wants you to wake up and pay attention, he'll do something crazy to you, like make you sick.

I'm actually under the weather right now as I write you this chapter. I like getting sick at times because it forces me to slow down. Smell the roses. Be grateful for the physical abilities I have when in full health.

I'm not talking about some serious illness here. I'm talking about the minor bug I get once in a while that zaps my energy and puts me on the couch for a few hours.

But I tell you what, those few hours without any desire to even think about work, or stress about the small things, force me to relax and help clean up my mental clutter.

As much as I advocate slowing down, finding balance, and assessing priorities, it's all much easier said than done.

I'm at the point in my life where I absolutely love everything that I do. I am fortunate to have my passions provide my paycheck, and rarely a day goes by where I feel like work is work. However, even with the best of intentions, sometimes work impedes my family and worship time. This is my cue. It's time to slow down. Cut stuff out. Regain balance. Remember this, no matter what you do you must not become consumed. Consumption isn't healthy. Balance is.

Usually when you're consumed, you are unable to meet the needs of those around you. You can't go outside of yourself. You're so bogged down in your own world that your blinders prevent you from seeing, feeling, and experiencing the world by your side.

I used to be consumed with myself, not realizing the effects of my consumption until I was able to release myself from their grip. I had obsessive tendencies, commonly referred to as OCD (Obsessive Compulsive Disorder). I say obsessive tendencies because I was technically never diagnosed with OCD, and fortunately it never got to the point where it severely impaired my functioning. Outside of my family no one witnessed my odd antics and nervous rituals, like opening and closing doors or turning on and off lights a certain number of times before entering or leaving a room. While at school or in public, much of the stuff was just in my head, like my aversion to certain numbers or my anxiety about my body type.

My OCD was a pain to handle, and most people didn't realize the severe emotional distress it caused. On the surface, I may have looked like a quiet kid, but in reality, my internal world was rocked with emotional turmoil. Quite often, I felt like I was going insane.

When the obsessiveness began revolving around my physique is when it really became obnoxious. I used to drop down and do twenty sit ups because I thought my abs were going to change after one meal. I considered myself fat at only 103lbs. If someone touched my chest muscles I thought they were going to flatten out. That's how irrational my thoughts were. I couldn't get over myself. I was so trapped in my own mental chaos that I wasn't fully seeing, feeling, or experiencing life and those around me. I realized the root was selfishness. It wasn't until I identified this that my mental exhaustion started clearing up and I began to find balance.

That's why it's so important for you to invest time into digging deep and finding yourself. Inner balance came for me when I started journaling, reading, praying, and giving myself quiet time to figure out who I was, how I got here, where I was going, and how I was going to get there.

Here are four things I want you to remember about Finding Balance and Keeping It:
1. DO NOT DO TOO MUCH OF ANYTHING
Too much of anything can become bad, even when it's good. You can eat healthy too much, you can work out too much, and you can even relax too much. Our nutrition philosophy is the 85/15 rule. You eat extremely

healthy for 85% of the time, and the other 15% you can eat absolutely whatever you want. To eat healthy 100% wouldn't be fun, and to be honest, it's not necessarily the best for your body. In fact, it's actually a fat-loss secret to eat crappy food periodically because the shock of unfamiliar garbage revs up your metabolism into high gear.

Exercising too much will burn you out, mentally and physically. You should never exercise every day of the week and in my opinion, you should take time off every three to four weeks. My typical cycle includes a week of either complete rest, or entirely different low impact workouts, every fourth or fifth week. Even the length of your workout itself shouldn't be too long. Keep it short and sweet and get out of there. This type of training will keep your mind and body fresh and your motivation as high as can be.

Even relaxing will get old after a while. One time our good friends took us to Arizona with them for a vacation. We hung out at the pool all day, ate food, and slept. It was such a refreshing and rejuvenating experience. But after ten days of doing it, I started to feel sluggish and unproductive. I knew it was time to get back in the routine of things. Vegging out is great, but go too long without physical and mental stimulation, and that's what you'll become — a vegetable.

2. TAKE A DAY OFF....AND THEN SOME

It's not a choice, it's a commandment. It's so important for your well-being, God actually mandates it in his Ten Commandments. Heck, even God rested. *"For in six days the LORD made the heavens and the earth, the sea and all that is in them, and rested on the seventh day; therefore the LORD blessed the Sabbath day and made it holy."* (Exodus 20: 11 NASB) Ideally, the Sabbath is observed on a Sunday, but realistically, because of your schedule, you may need to make it another day.

Do not take this lightly. When I say a day off, it means closed for business, shut down, no operation — no e-mails, phone calls, or thoughts related to work. Just retreat from your routine and relax.

Now, I also want to make a note here that this doesn't mean you work your life away the remaining six days. Rest has to be woven into your everyday existence. Be conscious of how much you work and entertain yourself. Some days you're going to work way too much but just be aware that you need to set aside time for yourself and your family. Other times you're going to be out with your buddies, but a week straight of doing that won't get you too far. Special occasions are understandable, but everyday occurrences aren't.

Rest isn't something to neglect. It will RESTore you to greatness. It's the seam between the world of work and the work of worship. It's what keeps us from unraveling.

3. PLAY. ALWAYS.

I'll never forget the theme song for Toys R Us (a toy department store). Part of the lyrics were, *"I don't' wanna grow up because if I did, I wouldn't be a Toys R Us kid."* It used to worry me. Growing up meant I couldn't play, and if growing up meant I couldn't play, then I didn't want to grow up! Well guess what, you don't have to. Just because you get older, that doesn't mean you have to lose your childlike heart. Never stop playing and never stop having fun.

I became very boring when I first started transforming from a punk college kid to a career focused adult. I thought that just because I was trying to straighten my life out meant I couldn't have fun. For me, this time of "fasting" from recreation and fun was necessary. There are times we need to fast from things in order to become fully conscious of our actions and intentions in order to change them. But having healthy fun, especially when the time is right, should never cease.

Even Jesus enjoyed having a good time. There's a popular story in the bible (John 2: 1-11) when Jesus attends a wedding in Cana at Galilee. The barrels of wine had become empty and the wedding party begins to worry. Mary, Jesus' mother, aware of his abilities, challenges him to refill the wine. Jesus orders the barrels to be filled with water. Although confused, His people obey.. Miraculously the water turns to wine. The Master of the banquet turns to the bridegroom and says *"Everyone brings out the choice wine first and then the cheaper wine after the guests have had too much to drink; but you have saved the best till now."* (John 2:10 NIV)

Jesus did this not to promote alcoholism, but to promote fellowship. People were having a great time together, and he wanted them to continue to spread the love. He enjoyed having a good time. He knew the importance of it for the health of the spirit.

4. ISOLATE

ISOLATION brings about REVELATION. To change your mind, you must have alone time with God. You have to escape the commotion to put your wheels in motion. What will be revealed is His purpose for your life.

This looks different for everyone. For some it's turning off the television and sitting quietly instead. For others it's writing in their journal for a few minutes before bed. Turning off the radio during your commute to work. Meditating upon waking before getting your day started. For me, it's going for a long workout with just me and my thoughts. All are ways to escape the chaos.

You'll think you don't have time, but then you'll remember that there are twenty-four hours in a single day. You can make the time. You'll think it's not going to work. But stopping yourself before you try won't either. You'll question the need, but then you'll find out, that even JESUS took the time. Luke 5:16 points out that *"Jesus often withdrew to lonely places and prayed." "Very early in the morning, while it was still dark, Jesus withdrew to a solitary place to be alone with God and pray."* (Mark 1:35) *"He went to a mountain and spent the night in prayer."* (Luke 6:12) After He fed the 5,000, He withdraws to be alone with God. Before He goes to the cross, He withdraws in the garden to be alone with God.

Jesus escapes to be with God. He doesn't let His busy schedule get in the way. His work doesn't take precedence. His ego doesn't either. He values the importance of isolation because it brings Him closer to His Father.

And He says to us, *"Here's what I want you to do: Find a quiet, secluded place so you won't be tempted to role-play before God. Just be there as simply and honestly as you can manage. The focus will shift from you to God, and you will begin to sense his grace."* (Matt 6:6 The MSG)

Life is not about you. We know that God works in mysterious ways, and we also know that the body does. Pain and sickness are sometimes signals to that body that it's done too much. It's time to shut down and rest before we go into overload and serious complications arise.

I love you, son. I believe in you. Now find balance today. It's an absolute game-changer.

THE UNCOMMON WORKOUT

*"God grants us an uncommon life to the degree
we surrender our common one."* — *Max Lucado*

*Some people make things happen, some people watch things happen,
some people ask what happened?* — *Unkown*

A group of people walk into a workout. One of them is my good friend, and two-time NCAA qualifying wrestler, Marcus Effner. Wrestlers are in great shape period. But this guy, he takes it to a whole new level. At the end of the workout he lies on the ground in exhaustion, others are walking out as if they just walked in. He is covered in sweat, some barely broke one. Most have already captured their breath, Marcus is barely breathing.

Same moves. Same circuit. Same routine. Why do some stroll out untouched while one of the best Division One college wrestlers still lie limp? Intensity. Some know how to dial it up, while others still struggle to turn the knob.

We have a saying at our gym: "A workout is only as hard as you make it." What you put into it determines the results, effectiveness, and outcome of your desired goals. You control the dial, the intensity, and the intention you put behind it. Same goes for life. And generally, you can hold nothing or no one else accountable for what you make of it, or don't.

There are two types of people in this world: those who live and those who merely exist. Both are a choice.

Those who choose to exist stand on the sidelines, they go through the motions, they wait for things to happen. Those who choose to live get in the game, take action, and make things happen.

Those who live are uncommon. The Apostle Paul was uncommon. Before he knew Jesus he murdered Christians. Then on his trip to the City of Damascus, Jesus stopped him in his tracks and took his sight away, exchanging it for a brighter vision—one of love, respect, and faith in Him. Paul then became one of the biggest ambassadors of the Christian faith. He didn't just talk, he walked. He got beat up, pummeled, thrown in jail and out of towns, but he got back up and walked in them again.

This story floors me. *"Then some Jews from Antioch and Iconium caught up with them and turned the fickle crowd against them [Paul and Barnabas]. They beat Paul unconscious, dragged him outside the town and left him for dead. But as the disciples gathered around him, HE CAME TO AND GOT UP. He went back into town and the next day left with Barnabas for Derbe."* (Acts 14:19-20, The MSG)

Paul's perseverance to share the Gospel with thousands of people is why Jesus hand-picked him to be one of His leading apostles. He became one of the most popular too. Paul scripted more words in the bible than any other any other author. Of the 27 books in the New Testament, he wrote 13 of them. He went against the grain. He was big on reflection and retraining one's mindset. One of my favorite verses comes from him, *"Do not conform to the pattern of this world, but be transformed by the renewing of your mind. Then you will be able to test and approve what God's will is—his good, pleasing, and perfect will."* (Romans 12:2)

As I think about Paul, I think of a great way to keep your mind renewed. I call it the *Uncommon Workout*. It has nothing to do with fitness, and everything to do with mapping out the course of your life.

THE UNCOMMON WORKOUT
ESTIMATED LENGTH: 60 minutes

PRESCRIPTION: Quarterly (Four times per year)

1. The Warm-up: Reflection
First, reflect on the last few months. What have you accomplished so

far? What were some transformative moments? What new things have you learned? How have you grown? This can be fun and a major confidence booster.

2. The Strength Circuit: Evaluation
Next, write down what areas you're slacking in and where you need to get better. This part isn't much fun. Checking yourself never really is—but it's necessary if you want to get moving in the right direction.

3. The Finisher: Designation
Finally, map out the following four areas of your life and designate at least one task for each that you hope to accomplish before the quarter is over. These are examples from my list this year.

    a. **Personal**: Finish in the top fifty in the Men's Health Urbanathlon on Oct 13.

    b. **Family**: Start our own Sunday family dinners that were so paramount when I was growing up.

    c. **Work**: Add 200 people to our blog list so we can continue to reach as many lives as possible.

    d. **Faith**: Create a prayer list for family and friends and our Fit Me Up family... and actually put it to use every day.

The *Uncommon Workout* keeps you on track. It's your action plan. Without doing it, you may lose sight of where you're going, and fall into the trap of mere existence. Thankfully Paul didn't fall. He admits he didn't have it easy. *"Three times I was beaten with rods, once I was pelted with stones, three times I was shipwrecked. Once I spent a night and a day in the open sea."* (2 Corinthians 11:25 NIV) But he kept plowing forward because he served something greater than himself, and he knew life wasn't about him.

Being uncommon requires taking the path of most resistance. It's not easy. But whoever said living was? Plus, no great endeavors were ever achieved, no legacy was ever left, no stories worth reading were ever written about a man or woman who was common.

Life is not about you. Hit the *Uncommon Workout today*. You may just find yourself face-planted on a gym floor after a conditioning session or in a jail cell after a preaching session. Either way, you know some impact was created to get you there. And that, my son, is being one who truly lives.

I love you, son. I believe in you. Now get out there and be uncommon today. It's an absolute game-changer.

PULL-UPS FOR ZOË

———

Fifty-two pills a day. Therapeutic vest treatments routinely. Nebulizer treatments regularly. Multiple hospital stays annually. It's not something anyone should have to endure, let alone a child.

Meet Zoe, sixteen years old. She Does. Diagnosed with Cystic Fibrosis at only a few days old, she's lucky to be alive. At the time of her birth, only two states screened for cystic fibrosis at infancy. She happened to live in one of them. The doctors were able to detect it. We're thankful they did.

Cystic Fibrosis is a rare and chronic disease that affects the lungs and digestive system of about 30,000 children in the United States (CF Foundation). The disease causes thick, sticky mucus to form in the lungs, digestive tract, and other areas of the body. People with CF have to deal with life-threatening lung infections, pancreatic issues that affect the absorption of food, persistent coughing or wheezing or shortness of breath, and many other issues. The CF Foundation reports that the median life expectancy for someone with CF is mid to late thirties.

I can say this, CF may try to take years away from Zoë's life, but she has way more life to her years than most people I know. She has a magical spirit to her. Within minutes of being in her presence you quickly sense something special. Her attitude says everything.

She's a positive person.
She doesn't see herself as any less fortunate than anyone else. She doesn't want pity. She sees life as a beautiful opportunity that she plans to enjoy.

She's determined.
She's a competitive cheerleader, performing flips and twists and jumps

and extreme balance holds. Her routines are demanding and after going max throttle for two minutes, she's literally pulled off stage to recoup for ten. With only 50% lung capacity she says this is good by the way, since she used to only have 38%), her oxygen is used up much more quickly than normal and takes much longer to replenish. Zoë knows the pain that follows her routines, but she goes hard anyway. She wants to give it her best effort no matter the consequences.

She cares for others.

Two years ago she spent five months in the hospital. That's a long time to sit by yourself in your room because your body can't be exposed to germs from other patients. She looks around. The hospital floor she resides on (RBC 5) is not very comfortable or pleasant. She links the effects this has on one's recovery. If the kids on her unit were in a colorful, up-to-date, cozy environment, they would be happier, healthier, and recover stronger. She starts to dream big. She begins to ask questions. She takes action. Soon the "Make A Wish Foundation" walks through her doors.

Sitting in front of them, Zoe could have asked for a trip to Disney World. She could have requested tickets to the next rock concert concert. She could have begged for the newest phone or computer. But instead her wish was to renovate RBC 5, to make it a more pleasurable environment for all the children who regularly stay there. Zoë put other people before herself. She gets what this life is all about.

That's when we stepped in. After hearing her story, I was compelled to help. I had a vision of doing pull-ups for a fundraiser, and now here was my cause. It made perfect sense. So on Saturday, February 9, 2013, we held *Pull Ups for Zoë*, a world record attempt for the most pull-ups in twenty-four hours to raise money and awareness for Zoë's dream and for cystic fibrosis research. It's what we called an ActivPrayer. I gave myself, my thoughts, my energy, my prayers, all to Zoë while performing pull-ups all day. We also held a team pull-up competition and a benefit party with food and raffles. It was one of the most incredible nights we've ever experienced.

We raised $29,000 in just four weeks. Even though I failed at my attempt and stopped at only 2,501 pull-ups—the record is 4,027—the day was a huge success.

Here's a recap of that special day from an excerpt I wrote about my experience in the trenches:

PULL-UPS BY NUMBERS

Saturday was an incredible night, possibly THE most incredible one I've ever experienced. Numerous people have told me that their lives were changed forever, and that they'll never forget it: that they wish others were in that gym with them.

I want to be completely honest. I woke up on Sunday feeling like a failure for missing my mark. I tell you this not to earn pity but to be real. This is what the mind will do when you put yourself out there. But then you shut it down by thinking of this fundamental message, LIFE IS NOT ABOUT YOU.

And you think about all the things it is about… 15 ½ hours of game-changing moments in the pit.

2,501 Pull-ups.

$25,000 raised.

20+ sponsors.

50+ volunteers.

400+ donors.

Three months ago feeling Zoë's spirit through another person's words.

Nine words from CJ Tinline, *"You should hear what this one girl wished for."* He said more, but no more were needed. I knew this was the child we needed to do this for.

One call came.

Four calls to her parents, 1 meeting.

Thirty-six days later and here we are.

6:45am I walk through those gym doors.

Zero expectations. I walk calmly and peacefully in God's security, not mine. I'm not sure how we got here or what's going to happen. I just know I was called and I followed. The rest is HIStory.

When called, FOLLOW. That's not easy to do.

Six years ago I wouldn't have. But today I lead with a different mindset: God doesn't call the qualified, He qualifies the called. He doesn't choose the equipped, He equips the chosen.

Seven hundred reps result in blisters. We quickly figure out a solution. Lesson: God will guide you.

One thousand reps cruised through in 3 hours and 9 minutes.

Thirteen hundred reps put me in a vulnerable position. Somewhere along the way I neglected proper hydration and nutrition. My body wore down. Severe tightness in my shoulders and arms, energy plummeted, and so did my mind.

It was time to FIGHT, and enjoy it.

James 1:2-5 Says, *"Consider it pure joy my brothers and sisters, whenever you face trials of many kinds, because you know that the testing of your faith produces perseverance."* This is a fierce battle, what could possibly be enjoyed?

Fourteen plus members from the Pit Crew. The Pit Crew was my team of brothers and sisters who stayed by my side all day. It was insanely humbling. My big brother Ryan and David Jack didn't leave me for 15 ½ hours. Neither did Dan Bednar, Tim Sweany, Chris Brown, Dave Anthony, Brian Reid, Brian Stout, and so many others. They called in Matt and Eric and Kathy to massage and tape up my back and arms. When I needed prayers, they huddled around me. Water and food, they fed me. Motivation, they pulled up with me.

Pit crews, everybody needs them. I didn't think I did. But without them I would have crashed and burned completely. They got me back on track so I didn't quit.

Not dead, can't quit. Multiple times I wanted to.

Seventeen hundred reps and I knew the record wouldn't be broken. A call to an ambulance seemed comforting, but I rested on this, *"I can do all things through Christ who strengthens me"* (Phil 4:13). Keep pulling up.

Six pm, barely two reps at a time. What's the point? I'm letting people down, what a chump.

2013 motto: LIFE IS NOT ABOUT YOU. Do you believe it, Theo? There's a girl here who you're sacrificing your time for, you think you have it bad: You wake up and think about what you're going to eat for breakfast. Zoë wakes up and puts on her vest for treatment. You think about the workout you'll do at the gym later. She wonders if she'll get an infection that will put her in the hospital again for the next 3 weeks. You take your breathing for granted. The phlegm in her respiratory system causes her to feel every breath. Zoë faces challenges every day. You're not doing anything compared to what she goes through. Get your butt back up and start pulling.

Twenty-three hundred reps I FIND THE WHY. I preach WHY WE TRAIN: for a better reason, for something more than our own life, for a greater cause. This was my ActivPrayer for Zoë. I was here to serve and dedicate to her my time, prayers, and energy to the entire day, and even weeks leading up to it. She was on the forefront of my mind all day. But another WHY was happening. Here I am completely finished, literally on my hands and knees praying for guidance and clarity on what to do next. A song came on. The verses on the wall appeared again.

God wants me in this place. He doesn't want a record to be broken; he wants me to be broken.

With no energy, no reserves, no mobility, and no strength to pull anymore, I completely and utterly rely on Him.

The scene from Passion of Christ pops into my head when Jesus literally crawls to put himself on the cross. After 6 hours of whippings, lashings, and torture, he hung for me. He didn't have to, but he did. The least I could do is follow his example and get back up to hang for Zoë.

Twenty-four hundred reps I face the crowd.

Six resurrection reps out of nowhere.

Two hours left of meaningful ActivPrayer.

One embracing hug from Zoë that will last forever.

Twenty of my kids surrounding the caution tape cheering.

Four final reps on the bar with Zoë. A perfect ending to a perfect day.

Because He spread his love to us; we can spread ours to Zoë; and now she can continue spreading it to so many. That's what *Pull Ups for Zoë* was all about.

Countless lives were changed and will continue to be changed from this event. For years to come children and families will feel something special on floor RBC 5 because of Zoë's renovation.

Life is not about you. You can use fitness to serve a greater cause with Intentionality, Meaning, and Purpose. Just wait for the call and follow.

It doesn't matter how hard you get knocked down, what matters is how fast you keep pulling yourself back up, and everyone out there with you.

I love you, son. I believe in you. Now get out there and pull up others today. It's an absolute game-changer.

RAISING A BOY TO BE A MAN

Step 1: Pick him up, hug him, kiss him, tell him you love him, and pray with him first thing in the morning.
Starting his day like this sets the tone in his world that he is loved, accepted, protected, and prepared to take on the rest of the world.

Step 2: Love his mother... and show it.
Be patient, be serving, be honoring, be compassionate, and be desperate for her 24/7/365, no matter what. Love her like Jesus loved the church. It's the best way to teach him how to treat a woman.

Step 3: Read books to him.
I neglected reading for most of my life. Incorporating it into my daily life has been one of the most powerful things I've ever done. Reading not only gives him knowledge, it gives him value for obtaining it. Not to mention it's one of the best ways to spend quality time with him.

"Teach your kids how to read and comprehend before anything. It equips them for life. For if they can do both, they can teach themselves how to do any-thing." (Taxi Cab Sensei, Chicago 2012)

Step 4: Pray with him: morning, meals, and night.
It's amazing how their attitude will shift after you pray together. At a very young age, kids get that there's something much bigger than them. It's never too early to show them how to give thanks, submit, and express love to the One who put him on this earth in the first place.

Proverbs 22:6 *"Train up a child in the way he should go; even when he is old he will not depart from it."*

Step 5: Cuddle him when he's sick.

These are times when he won't leave your lap. Comfort him. He needs to know he can rely on you for renewed strength and comfort through his weakness and pain. Just like our Father wraps his arms around us through sickness and in health, we should do the same for our children. *"Whenever we're sick and in bed, God becomes our nurse, nursing us back to health."* (Psalm 41:3 The MSG)

Step 6: Love first, teach second.

"Kids don't care what you know 'til they know that you care."
Don't let your ego get in the way. He hasn't seen, felt, experienced things the same way you do. Holding high standards, pushing him out of his comfort zone, setting firm guidelines is one thing. The emotion and intent behind it is another... and everything. *"But knowledge PUFFS up while LOVE builds up."* (1 Cor. 8:1) Your knowledge won't do anything if you're attacking him with it.

Step 7: Repeat this phrase, "I love watching you when you. . ."

Make this a staple statement in your vocabulary. During sports. At home. For school. When he tries. His performance will excel when he knows that you notice his efforts — not that you care that he won, not that you were disappointed that he messed up — but that you just love to watch him do what he does and display the person that he is.

Life is not about you.

I love you, son. I believe in you. Now raise your boy to be a man today. It's an absolute game-changer.

97 KISSES A DAY

—

Ninety seven Kisses.

That's how many I gave you one day. I counted the ones on your face, your hands, and your feet. Multiple kisses in a row counted as one and I made sure to not kiss you extra just because I was counting. The last one smacked you on your forehead at night when you crawled on my chest to fall asleep.

You never slept in bed with us before, but this was a special day. No electric power. At a friend's house. New environment. You were scared, so we let you snuggle between us.

Hurricane Sandy shut our world down all day. No Internet. No work. No leaving our generator-powered friend's house.

I'm not going to lie, I struggle to slow down. When circumstances cancel my activities of daily living I think about what I had to do and will have to do, and it takes me some transition time to go from productive-mode to lounge around in pajama-mode.

Slowed down.

Unplugged.

Disconnected.

When it's planned, it's easy. When it's not, it can be anxiety producing, especially when you're cold. You can't cook meals or wash laundry; you keep turning on a light switch every time you go into a room, forgetting that lights, along with the stove, microwave, and DVD player require electricity to work.

So after I get over myself and remember that IT'S NOT ABOUT

ME and it is about being in the moment...

After I remember the city and utility workers spending overtime shifts away from their family to reinstate the comfort of ours...

And the many others who have it way worse than we ever will, who may have lost their lives in fact in other parts of the country...

I say who cares to all of this meaningless stuff that I fret, and I thank God for things like Hurricane Sandy. Because it forces me to STOP and do things like count the number of kisses I give my son in a day, and reflect on what I can learn from situations like this.

HERE ARE MY TWO TAKE-AWAYS
FROM HURRICANE SANDY:

1. People are generally good at heart; it just sometimes takes a natural disaster to see it.

It's easy for me to think that the world is cruel. We are surrounded by a lot of negative media, and we see many people hurting. You hear the story of the Youngstown drive-by that put a bullet through the head of a sleeping eight-year-old, killing him instantly; you watch the special report about the ruthless, barbaric, heartless men forcing innocent children into the sex trafficking industry; you wake up to the news story about a Colorado sociopath who walks into a movie theatre and fulfills the fairytale massacre he concocted in his head.

Why wouldn't we be jaded and cynical and at times want to shelter our kids from the world?

A lot of people are bad, but a lot are good as well. Natural disasters seem to bring them out. We work together at four-way stops that once use to be traffic lights; neighbors come out to pull trees off the street and trampolines off your roof; the houses with power invite those without to share in their warmth and comfort.

I'm not saying I'll necessarily let my guard down, but these little glimmers of good Samaritans encourage me to think twice before I judge the heart of humanity.

2. You don't have anything that can't be taken away in an instant.

I watched a pastor on television the other day ask this impactful question:

What do you have, that you really, really have, that can't be taken away in an instant? We upgrade our possessions, we chase higher salaries, we puff out our chests when we're promoted, and yet not one of these, not one thing, maintains any eternal value. To strive for these accomplishments is not the problem, it's the attachment to them that is.

I walk into my house to pack more belongings.
Where is the heat you used to produce?
Where are the lights you once shined?
You're not the same as I remember,
You're not even mine.

Bam. That's where I want to stay. Nothing is mine, not a thing. It's all for Him, by Him, and because of Him.

No material possession will walk with me through the gates of heaven. I won't be followed by a seventy-six-wheeler pulling our house and everything in it like the one NASA used to transport the space shuttle in California in 2013. God is not going to ask me the net worth of my business or pat me on the back for finishing my basement.

Appreciating our things is necessary. Being good stewards of our belongings is essential. But detaching from them is vital for a meaningful existence. Our possessions can be taken away, our relationship with God cannot. Perhaps that's a much more profitable investment.

Let's make it two hundred kisses—because if you ask your mom, she insists she kisses you just as much, if not more than I do. That's a lot of kisses. Keep this up and I think we can consider you bulletproof from any hurricane the world throws in your way.

Life is not about you. The hope is that when you get older you'll stop in your tracks long enough and often enough, even when not forced to, to give those two hundred kisses a day back to someone else. From there I think it's safe to say that this world starts to become a little bit better one kiss at a time.

I love you, son. I believe in you. Now get out there and give kisses to the ones you love today. It's an absolute game-changer.

WHAT IS LOVE

—

True Love is sitting with your wife in the delivery room—smelling, see-ing, and hearing things you never thought could possibly come from the human body—and growing closer together in the process. That sums up love right there. I say this because I write this chapter as your mom is prepping to give birth to your little sister. The epidural is in. The contractions are hammering. I sit here waiting through this next four-minute interval until she shouts for me to hold her hand again.

Love is a difficult subject to write about. Who am I to try it? I fail miserably at times. But I've learned so much about what it's not, that I'm really fine-tuning what it is.

There are many false misconceptions about this four-letter word. As a result, the divorce rate in the U.S. is very high. Of those marriages that stay intact, it is rare to find strong couples who genuinely have fulfilled relationships.

This country has more books, seminars, counseling, and resources on this topic, yet we seem to be failing miserably. That's because the stan-dards, definitions, and expectations are unrealistic. And we're not build-ing on the right foundation.

Let me first tell you what love is not: **Love is not dramatic.** If your communication looks like something you just watched on a talk show, music video, or soap opera, then you're just acting. Yelling, screaming, exaggerated mannerisms, overdone sappiness, and drawn-out emo-tions aren't indicators of romance. If your behavior looks like some-thing from a novel, then it's not real and you still have yet to find your life's true character.

Love is not a fairy tale. Movies and television shows promote it. Everyone strives to find it. No one ever gets their hands on a fairy tale love story. Because it's not reality. People don't sweep each other off their feet and take their problems away too. You're not going to enjoy luxury and comfort 100% of the time for the rest of your life without at least some conflict and issues. Sparks eventually stop flying if they're not based on the proper fire to keep them ignited.

Love is not perfect. The grass is never greener on the other side. You'll never find a person who does everything right and has no flaws. Because guess what, you don't either. A perfect relationship doesn't mean it's perfect. It means you love each other's imperfections perfectly.

Love is not easy. If you're not ready to work hard, then don't even try. Love is one of the most difficult disciplines to master. In fact, you never will. A mentor once said "when you think you've mastered something, you've mastered nothing." I say when you think you've mastered love then you're downright crazy. But you can definitely work extremely hard to come close.

Love is not objectifying. The female body is not an object; don't treat it like that. Your sensors will be heightened by bikini covered models on magazine racks and nude women exploited on the Internet. Don't succumb to the lies of mainstream beauty. Then you'll miss the real kind when it's staring you right in your eyes.

Love is not based on sex. It seems that every love story shows a couple getting it on after the first night of knowing each other. That's not love. End of story.

Love is not about you. Don't wait for love. Get out there and give it. The irony is it will come back tenfold.

Now let's look at my take on what love is.

Love is honest. Tell her what you like and don't like and let her do the same. This way you can work together on getting better. Being real and direct will always be respected more in the end, especially if your love is based on the right stuff, that is. If she asks you if she looks good in that red dress and she doesn't, don't say she does. That will come back to bite you in the rear. She'll never know when to trust you if she thinks you're just saying what she wants to hear. Even though the first few times will be hard, remember there's always a way to say it--Speak the truth in love. Your attitude affects your delivery. And your delivery affects her attitude. Step back and know where you're coming from. Then speak in a way so that she'll know where you are coming from too.

Love is tough. It's tough to love someone, because it hurts when things don't work out the way you want within the relationship and including the relationship itself. The closer you are, the more that can come in between you. So be careful because it can hurt more to love than it does to not love.

It's also necessary to be tough when you love someone. You're each other's rock, but you're also each other's slingshot. You can push each other harder because you have solid support to fall back on. Life is hard; it's not wise to let each other take it easy.

Love is relentless. Through the good and the bad, love doesn't give up. When communication isn't happening, just keep loving and eventually IT will. When you're just not feeling it, just keep loving and eventually YOU will. When she's not responding, just keep loving and eventually SHE will.

Love is prioritized. It comes first. Before you can teach anybody anything, you better love them first. People don't care what you know until they know that you care. Approach people without it, and you sound like a noisy gong or a clanging cymbal.

Love is the solution. If everyone loved each other, there would be no problems. Wars wouldn't start. Abuse and neglect would be unheard of. Pain and harm inflicted by another would never even be contemplated. Racist barriers would come crashing down. World hunger and poverty would be tackled. Financial schemes to take more from others would be obliterated. With love all things are possible.

Finally, let me tell you what to do with love.
What's better than to use the reference of all love references? The source that comes from the One who is love. The bible.

1. LOVE GOD FIRST

And he said to him, *"You shall love the Lord your God with all your heart and with all your soul and with all your mind."* (Matthew 22:37) It's not the greatest of the ten commandments for no reason. Your mom and I learned the importance of this early in our marriage. Imagine God as the top point of a triangle and you and your wife are the side points. If you keep your eyes on Him and rise toward Him, you will always keep walking with each other on the same path in the same direction with the same purpose. Plus, when you emphasize your intention towards Him, you'll end up with your direction towards others. The natural consequence is you'll be able to love each other much better.

2. LOVE YOUR WIFE LIKE CHRIST LOVED THE CHURCH (Eph 5:25)

This means you will sacrifice yourself for her like Jesus did for us. The Bible calls a husband and wife to submit to each other, and it's the responsibility of the man of the household to submit first. You'll have to be humble, not domineering. You don't control her, you share responsibilities. Nowhere in the Bible does it say a man should not do the dishes and the laundry because it's a woman's job. Man up and work together to get things done.

You do have to lead with strong hands though. Dive deep into your spiritual growth so you can help your family with theirs. Pray at dinner time. Pray before bed. Read Bible stories and apply it to current situations together. Most importantly, live the way a Christian should live.

3. LOVE YOUR NEIGHBORS AND YOUR ENEMIES

"You have heard that it was said, 'Love your neighbor and hate your enemy.' But I tell you, love your enemies and pray for those who persecute you." (Matthew 5:43-45) People will do things that you can't stand and don't agree with and live a life much unlike yours. Hate the sin, don't hate the sinner. God didn't give you the right to judge and condemn. So many Christians push non-believers away because they act as though this is in their power. Your Christian responsibility is to love all. Not just those that love you or those that believe and behave in the same way. Anyone can do that.

Again here I go thinking I know what love is. Then here comes your little sister. I had to drop the notepad because she came fast. Only one hour of contractions and twelve minutes of pushing. Your mother launched this five-pound little tike out quick. I had the privilege to pull her out. Now you have the honor to help hold her up. It's a crazy world out there, but with all of our love combined, I know we can do it.

Life is not about you. Love is life's primary requirement. Love God and love His people. The rest is just bonus.

I love you, son. I believe in you. Now get out there and love today. It's an absolute game-changer.

NEVER FORGET WHAT
YOUR MOTHER DID FOR YOU

There's a show on the History Channel called Stan Lee's Super humans. It's about human beings that employ superhuman strength and abilities that are quite often incomprehensible and unexplainable. I wonder when they're going to do a show on mothers.

It never fails. The second baby, and I'm blown away again. Sitting in the delivery room, watching the last nine months unfold, experiencing the welcoming of what seems like the impossible--the gift of life.

A lot of things had to happen to get us here. It's not easy to make babies. It's especially not easy to make a healthy one. As I grab Alana's head and arm and pull her out from her gooey world into an even gooier one, I'm grateful she made it.

And then the utmost respect for my wife and mom clicks on. How and why did you go through that? And how and why do I ever forget it?

Mothers get overlooked. I do it a lot. I see the woman standing in line at the grocery story with two children. I don't even think about the fact that her first child didn't make it. After hours of pushing she came out a stillborn. Imagine losing your baby an instant before you get to hold her. I can't. No wonder she's so tender with the children at her side.

Then there's the young lady that waits on us at the restaurant. As if two miscarriages weren't bad enough, after her third enters the world, his daddy exits. She thought he was a good man until it was time to man up and take care if a child. Now she fends by herself to provide as a single mother.

Or the story about our friends who tried for years without avail. Finally after hundreds of headaches and thousands of dollars, they are blessed with not one but two little life-changers.

Or our friend who literally almost gave birth in her car. The one who had three C-sections. The one who had twins, twice. The one who labored for two days. The one who pushed out nine pounds, without any meds, twice.

Countless stories. Countless wonder women perusing the aisles, walking the parks, working out in my own gym. We are surrounded by super humans. Do we recognize it? The birth of Alana allows me to.

Of course babies will do that. They change everything. Especially our perspective. I leave the hospital with a different perspective again. One filled with extreme gratitude for my mom, for my wife, and every lady who brings the next generation of teachers, preachers, leaders, and other game-changers into this world.

Your mom made a crazy comment not too long ago. She said, "Theo, you accomplish a lot of cool things. I don't. I wish I could do something cool one day." I say Amber—you just did something I could never do. The most amazing talent, gift, and ability on the face of this planet you possess. I don't care what I accomplish, it will never compare to the hours you spent in the hospital fulfilling the greatest purpose and miracle in the world. You grew another human being inside your body. You carried a sac and cord that provided all vital nutrients and protection throughout nine months, inside your body. You pushed what felt like a watermelon out of a very tiny space, from your body. Then you go on to produce and excrete milk to provide adequate fuel for her developing system, from your body. You are superhuman. That's a title not I, nor any man, could ever claim.

I'm calling the producers of that show. Before I see another man eating twenty-six poisonous scorpions, or letting a semi-truck drive over his stomach, or using his freakish sense of smell to find an object in a library of books, I want to see them showcase childbirth on the same level as Super Human. Tell me that wouldn't produce some stellar ratings.

Life is not about you.

I love you, son. I believe in you. Now never forget what your mother did for you today. It's an absolute game-changer.

FORGIVE TO LIVE

Some bad stuff happens to us. People hurt us. The past may abuse and use us. We lose someone. We're betrayed by someone. And it's hard to let go. Not letting go makes it hard—nearly impossible—to move forward.

I think the worst thing that could happen in life is to lose a child. I'm not sure I would ever move on or could or would forgive. The loss of a child is something no parent should ever have to experience. Our good friend Emily had to. She lost her daughter Sophie to brain cancer when she was only four years old.

Recently, Emily posted a gripping picture on the internet. It was the last picture of Sophie right after she passed. Emily was holding her tightly as she refused to let her go. This is the caption she posted next to the picture:

> "Childhood Cancer Awareness Month is over, but I won't stop fighting for the kids and their families. A Mom should never have to wonder what the last picture taken with her daughter will be like. As we approach the date 6 years ago that Sophie went to be with the Lord, I reflect on this last picture. She was cold, her spirit was gone. Yet I wanted to hold her forever. This picture sits on the unwashed night-gown that she was wearing when she took her last breath. I still keep it next to my bed."

I talked with Emily about forgiveness. She said that she did have to forgive, but it's extremely hard. She further stated, "I beg for forgiveness from God every day for all my faults so that someday I will be with Sophie again."

Emily is one of the most down to earth, genuine, kind-hearted people you'll ever meet. It's truly apparent that God is in her. That's why she can forgive. Because that's what He does.

Jesus stoops for people.

"But early the next morning he was back again at the Temple. A crowd soon gathered, and he sat down and taught them. As he was speaking, the teachers of religious law and the Pharisees brought a woman who had been caught in the act of adultery. They put her in front of the crowd. 'Teacher,' they said to Jesus, 'this woman was caught in the act of adultery. The law of Moses says to stone her. What do you say?'

"They were trying to trap him into saying something they could use against him, but Jesus stooped down and wrote in the dust with his finger. They kept demanding an answer, so he stood up again and said, 'All right, but let the one who has never sinned throw the first stone!' Then he stooped down again and wrote in the dust.

"When the accusers heard this, they slipped away one by one, beginning with the oldest, until only Jesus was left in the middle of the crowd with the woman. Then Jesus stood up again and said to the woman, 'Where are your accusers? Didn't even one of them condemn you?' 'No, Lord,' she said. And Jesus said, 'Neither do I. Go and sin no more.'" (John 8:2-11 NLT)

Jesus is forgiveness. He took our guilt to the hill of Calvary. We have no right to make people feel guilty.

Forgiveness doesn't give people the right to hurt you; it takes that right away.

Forgiveness is not passive weakness; it's massive strength. It releases your pain so you can heal. Harboring grudges and animosity and turmoil ultimately affects, hinders, and prohibits you. And usually, only you.

Being a forgiving person doesn't mean you can't check people and put them in their place. It doesn't mean you can't fight for your right or you can't start a cause like Emily did to help other families who are in the same situation as she was. This doesn't mean you can't pro-actively develop a solution to a current problem. It just means you're not going to let things that have hurt you infest, congest, and stress your heart and mind.

You can't live your entire life with a chip on your shoulder. That chip will turn into a strain. Eventually into chronic pain. Without actively releasing, it turns into scar tissue that you can't ever get rid of without severe medical attention.

As Jesus is hanging from the cross, he forgives the murderers below who hung him. He's up there in the first place because He forgives you.

Life is not about you. Jesus forgives so you can live. There's nothing too serious or any reason why in your life, you can't do the same.

I love you, son. I believe in you. Now get out there and forgive today. It's an absolute game-changer.

DAD'S MEMO

—

Dear Giovanni,

My love never fails.

Since the day of your conception I knew that. I cherished your speedy heart beat as I listened with my ear placed to your mother's navel. I marveled at your eyes and nose that I could see during the ultrasound. Everything about you was a gift. And I cherished it.

Upon your arrival, my life approached completion. I now had a responsibility that turned into a privilege. A motivation to build a legacy now being written. There was an immense confidence that came just from being your father.

As you get older, the days only get better. I watch your language develop, and motor skills, and personality too. "Proud" doesn't do justice for how I feel about you.

You need to know that this never changes. We will butt heads at times. Disagree. Not see eye-to-eye. Our communication may change, but my love never dies.

You will make choices that I don't agree with. Tension will rise. Voices may too. Our attitudes may change but my love is always new.

You will make mistakes. Some very big. Some ignorant. Some daring. Our demeanors may change, but I'll never stop caring.

My love never fails... other things will. Your attempts. Your tries. You may shoot for the stars but land short of the skies.

Your classmates, coworkers, teammates, and friends. Rare are those who will be true to the end.

But remember who will—the One who carried us all. In life you may trip, but He took the fall.

Bad things will happen. You'll get hurt, scraped, and bruised. Lean not on your own understanding to get lost and confused.

My love never fails... yours shouldn't either.

There are two things in life that are mainly required. Love God and His people, the rest will transpire.

For by grace you've been saved, no good works could be done. To change your status, from second to one.

What's done is done. He walked to the cross. He put himself on it. We gained from his loss.

I urge you to take that first step, and when you feel like giving up, you look at that cross and remember... He didn't. So take another one.

When you feel like making an excuse... look at that cross and remember that He never gave one.

When you feel like quitting, remember that if you're not dead, you can't... because even after hours of whippings and lashings and abuse, He never did.

You dig deep and remember what He did for you.
The sacrifice He made.
The second chance that He gave.
The words that He scripted.
And the life that He gifted.
As you read the phrases He wrote,
that you quote and devote,
Never forget what matters most.
To live and to breathe His passion for serving.
To wash others feet, even if undeserving.
To stoop for less fortunate
and forgive of your neighbors.
To judge and condemn were not put in your favor.
Eyes up and rise up and throw all the ties up.
The lies and insecurities that constantly bind up.

Unleash the potential and champ from within.
When you release the pain and grip from your sin.
Lukewarm doesn't cut it. Complacency's fired.
If you're not moving, then you're as good as a liar.
In God's army you're hired, equipped and required.
To jump on the front lines and fight 'til you're tired.
Sweat and perspire and grind to your core.
When the going gets tough, then you give it some more.
Because that's when you soar and score what's in store.
When you knock and He opens the door,
and you gain the freedom to want nothing more.
A rarity you are that a great Architect created,
Not once was your design ever debated.
Miraculously, intricately, elated, you're slated
For greatness beyond what you've ever rated.
With purpose and meaning, you were put on this land.
The prize that you strive for is to sit at His hand.
Go forth and approach life like you're dying.
Failure won't happen as long as you're trying.

The pressure is off, son. There's nothing holding you back from being who you were meant to. No matter what you say, what you do, or whom you become—I love you. I believe in you. Nothing will ever change that.

Life is not about you.

Now get out there and be the life-changer that you are today. Your family needs you. Your friends need you. The world needs you. And so does God.

Love Forever,
Your Dad

ABOUT COACH THEO

Coach Paul Theo is currently the owner and fitness coach for FMU Fitness, a youth fitness and adult training company located in Avon, Ohio. Coach Theo wrestled for most of his life from middle school through college. When done competing, he entered the social work field. After a few years in the social work profession, he and his wife Amber stepped out in faith to launch their fitness company. They haven't looked back since.

The core pillars of FMU Fitness are faith, fitness, nutrition, the mental game, and life. *"We practice what we preach, and we preach what we practice. We love God, our family, and all the people that we work with. We would do anything to take care of all of them."* — Coach Theo

For more information on Coach Theo and his programs, visit:

WWW.FMUFITNESS.COM
TWITTER @FIT ME UP
FACEBOOK.COM/PAULTHEO
YOUTUBE.COM/HARDCORETHEO
REEBOK.COM/THEO

www.ingramcontent.com/pod-product-compliance
Lightning Source LLC
Chambersburg PA
CBHW061826040426
42447CB00012B/2837